From Fate to Choice

In the 1990s private security patrols in public places were occurring in many areas of the UK and moving closer to that traditional domain of the public police – streets and neighbourhoods. Such a phenomenon was ripe for sociological enquiry and, accordingly, this book, originally published in 1995, provides a focused interpretation of six key concepts, each central to the equity debate on private policing. Data from three research sites in the UK are presented throughout the book in the form of case studies. Equity of justice is crucial and intrinsic to the association policing should have with a democratic, equal and free society. Private security, however, is not conducive to these requirements for it has an inherently competitive style excluding freedom from those who are non-competitive through either choice of economic disadvantage. Accordingly, an embarrassing characteristic of private security policing is that it promises too much freedom of choice in a less than equal world.

From Fate to Choice

Private Bobbies, Public Beat

Michael McManus

Routledge
Taylor & Francis Group

First published in 1995
by Avebury (Ashgate Publishing Ltd)

This edition first published in 2024 by Routledge
4 Park Square, Milton Park, Abingdon, Oxon, OX14 4RN

and by Routledge
605 Third Avenue, New York, NY 10017

Routledge is an imprint of the Taylor & Francis Group, an informa business

Publisher's Note
The publisher has gone to great lengths to ensure the quality of this reprint but points
out that some imperfections in the original copies may be apparent.

Disclaimer
The publisher has made every effort to trace copyright holders and welcomes
correspondence from those they have been unable to contact.

A Library of Congress record exists under ISBN: 1859720994

ISBN: 978-1-032-81715-6 (hbk)
ISBN: 978-1-003-50108-4 (ebk)
ISBN: 978-1-032-81725-5 (pbk)

Book DOI 10.4324/9781003501084

From Fate to Choice:
Private Bobbies, Public Beats

MICHAEL McMANUS

Research Fellow
Department of Sociology and Social Policy
University of Durham

Avebury

Aldershot • Brookfield USA • Hong Kong • Singapore • Sydney

Published by
Avebury
Ashgate Publishing Limited
Gower House
Croft Road
Aldershot
Hants GU11 3HR
England

Ashgate Publishing Company
Old Post Road
Brookfield
Vermont 05036
USA

British Library Cataloguing in Publication Data

McManus, Michael
        From Fate to Choice: Private Bobbies,
        Public Beats
        I. Title
        363.2
        ISBN 1 85972 099 4

Library of Congress Catalog Card Number: 95-76326

Printed and bound by Athenæum Press Ltd.,
Gateshead, Tyne & Wear.

Contents

Acknowledgements   vii

1   An introduction to an agency of social control   1

2   Research environments, methods and issues   16

3   The state and the market: contrasting views   31

4   Motives   59

5   Community and functional characteristics   75

6   Relationships   103

7   Crime control   110

8   Conclusions and policy implications   117

Bibliography   137

Index   158

For Annette, Devin and Leigh.

Acknowledgements

The research on which this book is based was made possible by the generous cooperation of several individuals and organizations and I would like to express my thanks to them. I am especially indebted to my Chief Constable, Mr. F. W. Taylor, Q.P.M. and the members of Durham Constabulary Police Committee for allowing me to undertake the study. I am also grateful to the Directing Staff of the Police College who supported the research by awarding me a Bramshill Fellowship - I acknowledge here the specific support and tutorship of David Pope. Thanks also to Dr. Nigel Fielding of Surrey University and Professor Richard Brown of Durham University and his staff at the Department of Sociology and Social Policy - in particular Dr. Bob Roshier and Dr. Dick Hobbs who patiently and professionally shared with me their intellect and excellent insight into the sociology of policing. The book was only made possible, however, by the subjects of the study - the public and private police and their clients. In this respect I wish to thank Tommy King, Ray and The Nighthawks, John Daly, Keith Morcomb, Jacky Ashenden, Nina Rueda, Metropolitan Police Officers Bromley and Orpington areas, Northumbria Police Officers Washington area and Durham Constabulary Officers at Pelton. Finally, thanks to Annette for her unending patience and understanding.

As it moves along its twisted course, capitalism requires an ever changing ensemble of strategies to meet new crises, and in the current period the 'remedy' is clearly based upon the 'privatization of profit' and the 'socialization of costs'.

Spitzer, 1983, p. 328

1 An introduction to an agency of social control

An important period in the history of policing provision is currently occurring in the United Kingdom. Residents in many neighbourhood areas, concerned with rising crime rates, have broken with tradition and turned to the private sector police for the provision of security patrol. This book is based on that change - from traditional public police security provision to private security provision of neighbourhood patrol. It is a change from fate to choice. As a public police officer, committed to providing public security, I wanted to explore the reasoning behind this current demand by some communities for enhanced security provision through the private sector police. This new and emerging phenomenon of private security patrol in neighbourhood areas is an interesting change to British policing - for these areas have been sovereign to the public sector police since at least 1829. Public police duties have been clearly defined over the years:

> It is indispensably necessary that he (the constable) should make himself perfectly acquainted with all the parts of his beat or section, with the streets, thoroughfares, courts and houses....He will be expected to possess such a knowledge of the inhabitants of each house, as will enable him to recognise their persons. He will thus prevent mistakes, and be enabled to render assistance to the inhabitants when called for......He should see every part of his beat in the time allotted; and this he will be expected to do regularly so that any person requiring assistance, by remaining in the same spot for that length of time, may be able to meet a Constable. (Metropolitan Police, 1836, p. 23).

And further:

The constable is responsible for the security of life and property within his beat, and the preservation of the peace and general good order during the time he is on duty. He should make himself perfectly acquainted with all parts of his beat, with the streets, thoroughfares, courts and houses. He should possess such a knowledge of the inhabitants of each house as to enable him to recognise them. He should visit, as far as possible, all the lanes, courts and alleys, and when going his rounds at night he should carefully examine all premises and see that the doors, windows, &c., are secure. (East Sussex Police, 1919, p. 16).

The association between the public police officer and the public places he/she patrols still remains a crucial aspect of police occupational culture today. The professional responsibility that the constable feels for life and property on his/her own 'patch' is a matter which is personally taken very seriously. The police officer tends to consider the British Police Service as having a monopoly over the provision of public protection - especially in respect of policing the streets. Central to this belief is the notion that clear distinctions exist between the public and the private spheres of policing and that one of the public agency's primary responsibilities is to ensure that it retains sovereignty over the crime problem (Henderson, 1987, p. 51).

Prior to the introduction of Robert Peel's new public police system in 1829 the inhabitants of the British Isles more or less policed themselves (Trevelyan, 1942, p. 230). The state gave little financial support to policing in those times - a system of common informers was relied upon and only a few constables were paid out of the fines of offenders. Policing provision then was primarily a private matter. After 1829 the method of policing was radically changed to a system of state provision financed by public taxes. Recently, however, one can discern a move back to those times of private justice - for security provision today is increasingly being provided by private agencies. Indeed, many individuals now consider that the most efficient and cost-effective way of policing is to expose security provision to competition through the market (Adam Smith Institute, 1989, 1991). Indeed, policing services can now be provided from a continuum which exists between the public and the private. This is especially obvious in the United States of America where state police contract-in private police for some state policing functions (Chaiken and Chaiken, 1987). It would now seem that the provision of policing services can no longer be assumed a rightful province of the state. This is because markets, enterprise and choice have once more become fashionable. Appropriately, Hirschman (1970, 1983) has suggested that a feature of western society is a shifting involvement from the private to the public sphere and back again.

Defining 'policing' and 'private security'

At this point it is appropriate to consider the concepts of 'policing' and 'private security' in more detail.

Policing

Policing is essentially concerned with social control. It is often executed against the will of individuals and groups and relates to both moral and physical assertion. The concept of policing has both a narrow and wide interpretation. We may use it in its narrow sense as merely the function of a civil force - e.g. the Police Service of England and Wales. This form of policing is associated with purely 'public' as opposed to 'private' policing. Public policing is most usually operated by employees of the state, is characteristically supported by taxation and organized on a bureaucratic basis. But this is a definition too restrictive for the present study. In contrast, a wider and less limited definition relates to the whole resources of civil administration - all government departments such as Health, Home Office, Social Security and Environment. Additionally we may add the entire population - for each of us has a duty at common law to uphold the peace and, although rarely used by ordinary citizens, arrest offenders against it. Furthermore, the mere action of an individual resident who peers out of the window at activity in the street is clearly a 'policing' activity within this wider definition. The combined policing efforts of private individuals, in contrast to purely state efforts, may be termed 'private policing' and often exists as part of a free market system - for example, where a private security company is contracted by a private individual or corporation to protect property. The services and functions of the private security industry can, thus, also be included within this wide umbrella of 'policing' (Shearing, Farnell and Stenning, 1980, p. 17).

Policing in this wider sense relates to a more sophisticated interpretation which can be extended even further for the essential purposes of the present study. It can be summed up as a whole cluster of practices and knowledge which are embedded at many points in the social field (Pasquino, 1978, p. 52) and which constitute a set of policing structures encompassing the whole of society. Indeed, it is quite clear that in Britain today this is the objective of the state concerning social control. This all-encompassing pattern of control may be seen by some as innocuous and a positive contribution to social control (Sherman, 1983; Henderson, op. cit.). In contrast, it may be seen negatively as a form of domination where the surveillance of individuals, through various means of information, reflects the

3

interdependence of the relationship between power and knowledge (Foucault, 1979a) and the partiality of justice in favour of the economically privileged (Hall and Scraton, 1981).

Private security

Private security could be defined as 'the sum total of all those preventative and protective efforts provided by entities other than government' (Gallati, 1983). This wide interpretation does not merely consider the efforts of the private security industry and its personnel (South, 1988) but all private actions taken to protect persons and property. Efforts provided by government agencies, such as those carried out by the Police Service, cannot be included within this definition. This restriction on public inputs assists the clarity of the definition while at the same time draws our attention to the need for a more sophisticated interpretation of public and private relationships. This is because the public police are very often concerned in initiating and co-ordinating schemes, e.g. Neighbourhood Watch , but which are primarily run through private efforts. Furthermore, the public police regularly advise private individuals on general methods of protection. Thereafter, those receiving advice, not the police, provide the means of protection. Neighbourhood Watch schemes and other protective strategies cannot, thus, be associated purely with 'private' security, unless their provision is totally removed from the influence of the Police Service. They must, therefore, normally lie somewhere between public and private security. Thus, interrelationships between the public and the private serve to blur purely public or private definitions of security. Where public and private territorial limits do not appear to have been drawn clearly, opportunities will exist for working relationships between public and private agencies. The end product of these relationships may well turn out to be a form of security provision which cannot be defined strictly as either public or private - a public/private security continuum exists (Shearing and Stenning, 1981, p. 196).

As the present study concerns private security personnel operating in both 'public' and 'private' places, a definition which focuses on those aspects is needed. This purpose is served by the interpretation provided by Kakalik and Wildhorn (1972) who describe private security as, 'private forces providing all types of security-related services including investigation, guard, patrol and armoured transportation'. An emphasis here is placed upon 'private forces' who provide a service. This is more specific and immediately brings to mind the private security industry as the provider. Private security thus defined is of two types: contract security is hired or supplied to the end-user by a company on some form of contractual basis, and in-house, or proprietary security, is hired directly by the end-user company as permanent full-time or part-time employees of that company (Siatt, 1981, p. 21).

A dearth of knowledge

In the traditional academic sense security is not a body of knowledge guided with a strong research base. Accordingly, the very limited empirical and theoretical knowledge concerning private security patrol in neighbourhoods, and its relationship to other institutions, provides an important and fundamental reason for undertaking this study. For, when the literature in this field has been examined it is apparent that there has not been an adequate conceptualization of these relationships (Henderson, op. cit., p. 56). As an academic subject the private security sector in general has attracted some interest and its existence has been under review for some years both in the United Kingdom (Home Office, 1979; South, 1985, 1988) and America (Shearing and Stenning, 1983). Empirical research carried out specifically on private security patrol in neighbourhoods, however, is hardly prolific - although there are political tracts on it which help in understanding the philosophy it is based upon. For instance, the fact that public policing is expensive in comparison to general government spending in other areas (Brewer et al, 1988, pp. 11-12) makes the ideology of active citizenship a matter for government to enthusiastically promote (Fielding, 1991, pp. 221-226).

In searching sociological and criminological abstracts, however, one is not likely to identify any empirical research in the United Kingdom, and only one study in the United States (Donovan and Walsh, 1986) which has examined this specific area of private security patrol in neighbourhoods. But the Donovan and Walsh study (ibid.) was wholly empirical and had not considered theoretical perspectives concerning the strategy's relationship with other institutions. When one considers the mass of empirical research carried out on neighbourhood 'public' police patrol the lack of research into 'private' security patrol is even more surprising. This paucity of knowledge must be seen against the fact that in some American cities the numbers of patrolling security personnel outnumber public police officers (Bayley, 1986, p. 216) and in the United Kingdom private security patrol is steadily increasing (Police Review, 1989b, pp. 118, 740, 1406; Operational Policing Review, 1990). Accordingly, there is a need to increase and develop academic knowledge on the general area of the private security sector and also to develop a conceptual perspective regarding the particular subject area of the present study.

Equality in policing provision: an ethical necessity

The primary aim of this book is to identify the nature and function of private security patrol in neighbourhoods relative to the extent of its equity and freedom as a system of policing. Secondary aims are to ascertain the accuracy of the thesis that the ineffectiveness of public police leads to the demand for private security patrol in neighbourhoods and, finally, to provide a general analysis of the fieldwork both in policy terms and with reference to socio-legal and police studies. In the final analysis this study shows how private security patrol in residential areas may or may not be conducive to the requirements of quality and equity of justice - requirements so crucial to the association policing should have with a democratic, equal and free society.

Provision of policing services through the market inevitably leads to an increase in individual and corporate choice. Whereas public systems of justice provision tend to be organized on a bureaucratic basis and provide services in which the recipient may have little choice concerning what will be supplied, private justice systems are less bureaucratic and more flexible - indeed they have inherent within them a relationship with purely choice principles of justice. This relationship between private justice and purely choice principles tends to increase the prominence of private actions. In this respect conservative ideology currently stresses the need to cut back on government provision of various public services and gives individuals more opportunity to choose their own forms of security. This ideology draws upon value themes that run deep in British society - beliefs about freedom of choice, the greater efficiency of the marketplace and the importance of self reliance and charity. Principles concerning choice are, thus, more closely associated with conservative ideology and private provision than they are with public provision.

This principle of choice in community policing has led to various forms of private provision where neighbours have voluntarily come together to solve crime problems. This may be seen as positive by conservatives, but for others the unequal starting points of individuals could easily lead to inequality of provision - for the rich can afford to pay for services which the poor cannot. Does private security patrol in neighbourhoods, therefore, serve as a form of class injustice leaving the less well-off, who have fewer resources and often greater need, in a less secure and hostile environment than those who have the economic power to purchase their security through the market? And to the extent that richer neighbourhoods are more likely to be better organized against crime through private resources, will that mean displacement and increased crime in adjacent, less well-off neighbourhoods? Such questions of distinction between public and private provision obviously impact upon the debate surrounding the morality and ethics of policing provision.

Private systems of policing, thus, bring into question ethical and moral principles concerning provision of services. Some distinctions have to be made between services which can be wholly influenced directly by the market and other services, such as health, education and public security, which may be so essential to public welfare that they should predominantly be provided by the state rather than left to market forces and individual choice. But the retention of the choice to buy or to depend on state provision is itself an important principle - for if that choice is lost then personal freedom may also be diminished. When there is no choice but to buy the social order is unjust and beyond standards of human decency - since the poor are denied essential state protection. There is little to be gained by such people in belonging to an organized society (Alderson, 1991, p. 42).

These matters can only be addressed through posing questions about power: by whom is it exercised, over whom and by what means? And the answers to these questions can be given by analysing power on a continuum which has as its polar opposites the concepts of freedom and oppression as they relate to policing. Thus, by identifying the sources of power in this study the contemporary position of policing in the United Kingdom, and its relationship with the private sector and the state, will be described in microcosm. In relation to the overall fairness of justice systems, this area of research generates important administrative and academic questions concerning the 'carriers' (Berger, Berger and Kellner, 1974) and direction of social control in contemporary British society.

At this stage we can briefly touch upon some theoretical aspects concerning community policing, including the thesis that private security in such locations tends towards inequality of provision - interestingly, a thesis with few conclusive empirical illustrations to support it.

Blurred and sinister boundaries?

The move from private to public justice in the latter half of the eighteenth century (Critchley, 1978; South, 1987a) created the possibility of 'blurred boundaries' where state and citizen merged to provide policing services - a possibility supported by the notion that in a capitalist system public policing never fully replaces private policing (Bayley, op. cit., p. 37). It has been argued that the apparent recent move towards private forms of justice is likely to allow injustice (South, op. cit., p. 106) and that the private security industry in particular is a biased and selective form of policing (South, 1988, p. 155). Such an interpretation regards moves towards the private as having sinister consequences for equality and for freedom from an overbearing policing system. Bottoms, (1983, p. 192) however, has shown this claim of 'sinister blurring' to be highly questionable. Some American research does tend to support the notion that a move away from public towards private sector justice may reduce the quality of provision. Pascal and Menchik, (1979) for instance, found that a leaner and smaller public sector may also turn out to be meaner and harsher for the less privileged. That research was supported by the work of Walker, Chaiken, Jiga and Pollin (1980) who found that public police departments concentrated their resources away from crimes which had a low probability of detection and, in relation to property crime, a low value financially. This trend in 'screening', which currently occurs in the United Kingdom, could be interpreted as either an improvement in efficiency of resources or a disturbing philosophical shift in the role of the public police who hitherto applied their services equally over the broad spectrum of crime. Apart from the fact that these research findings cast doubt upon the ability of the public police to bring any substantial reduction in crime rates, it also helps us to understand how individual complainants, and indeed whole neighbourhoods, may look to the private sector police to resolve the problems which the public police screen out.

The increase in the demand for private police can be seen in a broader sense through the concern of some writers for the phenomenon of 'community penetration' - for example the notion that formal, state agencies of social control pierce and absorb the informal networks of society (Cohen, 1985). Others experience uneasiness that external control systems, such as the private security sector, are gradually expanding (Mathiesen, 1983). These concerns are represented in the 'dispersal of discipline' thesis - the idea that the state has created an extension of social control into social institutions, agencies and spheres of life - some of which, like the family, (Donzelot, 1979) are not formally identified with control at all. There is an important need to discover how accurate this analysis of blurred and sinister policing boundaries is when applied to private security patrol. If there is empirical evidence to be found in support of the theory of these left-functionalist writers it could not be found any closer to the freedom and equality of individuals than within their own families (Donzelot, ibid.) and, in the case of the present study, their own neighbourhoods and streets. Using the subject of private security patrol as a research base allows an

8

investigation into the apparent imbalance towards those left-functionalist explanations of private police (Shearing and Stenning, 1987a) which argue the existence of a predominantly disciplinary (Foucault, op. cit.) and sinister (Cohen, S. 1979) form of control which impacts upon equality of provision and freedom from repressive policing systems.

Public inability equals private opportunity?

A secondary aim of this study is to consider any association which may exist between the ineffectiveness of public police patrol to control crime and the introduction of private security patrol in neighbourhoods. Crime has become a predominant social problem within most western societies and when citizens experience crime in their neighbourhoods the problem becomes more focused for them - and they usually look first to the public police to resolve matters. But there are problems associated with public expectations of the police. Although it is recognized that massive increases have been made to police budgets in recent years, there is still a shortfall in what is being provided to effectively prevent and detect the majority of offences. The demand for police response has certainly overtaken the level of police resources available and police in many areas cannot now provide the level of service demanded. Analyses of why this has occurred have come to various conclusions, including purely budgetary constraints (O'Connor, 1973) and lack of technological resources to better manage crime (Albanese, 1986, pp. 86-87). This inability of the public police to effectively perform the tasks expected of them has been associated with the reasoning for the introduction of private security patrol in neighbourhoods (Slynn, 1983; Albanese, ibid.). The present study, therefore, aims at measuring the accuracy or inaccuracy of the hypothesis that inadequate public police provision in neighbourhoods influences the introduction of private security patrol.

It could easily, however, be argued that there are other reasons than police ineffectiveness which have led to an increase in neighbourhood security patrols. Foremost amongst alternative explanations may be the rapid increase in the number of private agencies now available (Randall and Hamilton, 1972; Shearing and Stenning, 1981; South, op. cit., pp. 23-34) and easy public access to them through the media (Mathiesen, 1987, p. 74). Furthermore, mere increased access to private agencies may simply prompt individuals in capitalist societies to react to an inherent human need for more security (Spitzer, 1987, p. 50).

Theoretical analysis: relational argument and evaluation

It is important to set the scene early for the ensuing theoretical discussion which will follow the empirical analysis of the fieldwork in this study. Contrasting and diametrically opposed views, policies and ideologies on community crime control and police and state relationships are critically and thoroughly explored throughout the book. Particular claims and assumptions made in the opposing arguments are focused upon so that accuracy can be measured against the subsequent findings and analysis of the fieldwork. In order to achieve this objective it is first necessary to present a preliminary overview which will identify the dominant contemporary theoretical position in which the notion of private police is legitimized. Thereafter, a theoretically dominant antithesis will be presented. Thus, two contrasting theoretical perspectives on the state and crime control will be assembled - both primarily located within the sociology of social control and punishment. Critical assessments of these perspectives are made throughout the study to confirm, modify or reject particular claims. The conceptual background which is developed assists in formulating important research questions and helps to establish the choice of design for methods used in the fieldwork. The final analysis of the study will provide conclusions which are based upon reasoned, conditional commitment to a perspective which best describes the empirical findings.

Dominant perspectives

The theoretical overview which follows is derived from the work of several writers on social control and the state in capitalist societies. The use of a range of theories - 'theoretical triangulation' - is here applied to complement the study, (Denzin, 1970) for it is very unlikely that any study clearly supports one specific proposition. Triangulation, therefore, allows systematic and continuous interchange between theory and research (Jupp, 1989, p. 83). In this respect I use the Liberal Democratic social control theory of Neo-Classicism and contrast it with antithetical and critical theories of 'Capitalist Logic', 'Commodity Fetishism' and 'Dispersal'. The strength of the theorists used here lies in their integration of a number of different approaches and the way they make sense of the contemporary social scene - variations in strategies of surveillance dependent on the social status of the subject population; the state's use of new surveillance strategies to prevent deviance; the way that new professions seek to exploit this usage and the ways that the public themselves seek out control, guidance and security from experts. As ideal-type paradigms these antithetical approaches may be seen as Classicist and Marxist (Young, 1981, pp. 253-266, 294-305). The purpose of setting up ideal types is to help develop concepts which may prove to have systematic import. But it must be remembered that conceptualization based upon broad bipolar distinctions derives from phenomena which are not directly observable. The device is, therefore, merely analytical and has no empirical basis.

The newly emerging strategy of private security patrol is consistent with two theoretical models in crime prevention, namely 'informal social control' (Jacobs, 1961; Wilson and Kelling, 1982) and 'opportunity reduction'. These are located within the Classicist approach to control. Informal social control came to popularity in the 1970's when research and policy shifted from offender based explanations of crime to preventing offences in the community (Hope and Shaw, 1988, p. 8). This situational approach to crime prevention continued to have an important influence on criminal justice policy in the 1980's (Clarke and Mayhew, 1980; Heal and Laycock, 1986) and remains so in the 1990's. The situational approach, and its emphasis upon the intended or unintended consequences of purposeful human action, portrays a particular theoretical representation of the state which, in the 1990's, is clearly associated with The New Right in politics (Dunleavy and O'Leary, 1987, p. 91). The approach can conjure up notions of dictatorship and oppression and by its intrusiveness may be seen as a threat to individual liberty (Shearing and Stenning, 1987a, 1987b; Sherman, op. cit.; Klein and Luxenburg, 1987; Klein, Luxenburg and King, 1989). These contrasting approaches are now further developed separately and analysed in relation to the state.

Liberal democratic theory and the dominant perspective: neo-classicism and the enabling state

Liberal-democratic theory is predicated upon the assumption that in modern capitalist societies the law and politics are divorced from the direct influence of economic interests - the legitimacy of the state and the law lies with the consent of the people. Justice is impartial and gives no advantage to those who own or manage the economic system. This notion of separation from direct political power - rich and poor alike are equal in the sight of the law - is seriously contested (Hall and Scraton, op. cit., pp. 470-471). The present policy dominating crime control in Europe and America has its roots in this theory and can be traced from that which developed in the late eighteenth century out of the Philosophy of the Enlightenment and which is termed 'classicist' (Young, op. cit., p. 253; Roshier, 1989). In contemporary British

11

and North American society an amalgam of classicist and positivist thought has emerged into the dominant criminological paradigm of neo-classicism (Radzinowicz, 1956; Cohen, 1981; Young, op. cit.). Thus, classicist and neo-classicist thought is closely associated with notions of societal consensus, freedom of choice, a free market and deterrence based on 'social contract theory' (Clarke, 1980; Wilson, 1983). These voluntaristic tendencies of classicism are inherent also in neo-conservative ideology, (Dunleavy and O'Leary, op. cit.) save that in the latter, tension in human action remains unresolved (Young, op. cit., p. 275).

The neo-conservative debate on freedom of choice and on effectiveness and efficiency has adherents in many parts of the criminal justice system (Savas, 1983; Wilson, op. cit.; Henderson, op. cit.). Such writers all share common opinions - the idea of causes of crime as 'determined' is antagonistic and they show a lack of interest in aetiology. Belief in choice in the human act is, however, dominant in neo-conservatism - hence, deterrence is advocated. There is little that public policy can do in the region of psychological causes of crime and the idea of reform is discarded with the notion that crime can be affected by improving social justice (Clarke, ibid., pp. 9-11). The goal of social policy, therefore, must be to build up effective deterrents. Non-state welfare organizations in the private sector are to be invoked - the public themselves and the private security sector.

For some of these commentators the Anti-Collectivist age has arrived (George and Wilding, 1985) as conservative governments in Britain, Canada (Guest, 1984) and the U.S.A. (Weddell, 1986) roll back the boundaries of state provision. This 'enabling' state concept (Power, 1987; Ridley, 1988; Gilbert and Gilbert, 1989) is seen as part of the 'Neo-Conservative Dream' to replace the Welfare State and create the 'Dawn of the New Enlightenment' wherein education, housing, local government finance, health and community care legislation is passed to 'embody the first real advance of new Libertarian ideas into social policy status' (Glennerster, Power and Travers, 1991). The nature of this move towards a more enabling state is distinctly ideological in that it represents the possibility of inequality of service to those who are unable, or merely choose not to pay for private services. It may not, however, be inevitable that privatization itself will lead to inequalities. Rather, it is the political and social values intensifying the move towards privatization which are likely to create an inequitable justice system (O'Higgins, 1987).

For Anti-Collectivists their core value of 'freedom', as it applies to choice, has a close interrelationship with a market economy. But as 'inequality' is also a core value of their beliefs (George and Wilding, ibid.) equality of justice is impossible. As well as holding the belief that the pursuit of

12

egalitarian policies is incompatible with freedom (Hayek, 1949, p. 22) there is also a view that this enabling 'minimal' state concept is anything but what it appears. Rather than contracting there is a view that the state expands through delegation and devolution (Cohen, 1985). For example, Neighbourhood Watch, as a private form of policing, would be interpreted as supplementing state police manpower, and consequently strengthening state power.

The critical perspective: the oppressive state

The privatization debate has prompted some writers to argue that whereas policing used to occupy a legal enclave by enforcing the law and thereafter 'excluding' offenders (in prisons and other total institutions) the state currently tends to reach out and befriend - to become community based. A new epoch in the structure of social control has been entered by a contemporary shift from an individual to a collective form of social control (Mathiesen, 1983, p. 139). Here the traditional boundary between police and community - the public and the private - is becoming increasingly blurred (Cohen, ibid., Chapter 2). These writers tend to align to a left-functionalist position and seek to identify the repressive, coercive and sinister nature of the state and of conventional criminal justice strategies. The ultimate nightmare for these writers is an entirely pervasive state wherein the community becomes the primary means of repression, by either excluding strangers or by various forms of surveillance (Foucault, op. cit.; Garland and Young, 1983; Cohen and Scull, 1983; Cohen, 1985; Lowman, Menzies and Palys, 1987; Shearing and Stenning, 1987a, 1987b). Thus, the principles of 'equality' and 'liberty' are key factors of dispute within the critical debate on private policing and are seen by left functionalists as sources of contradiction in a capitalist system.

In contrast to the classicist perspective, these opposing left-functionalist views reflect a distrust and lack of confidence in the formal criminal justice system. Explanations and alternatives are sought in the control systems of pre-modern societies (Spitzer and Scull, 1977a, 1977b; South, 1987a) and there is a bias towards explaining social change purely in economic terms (Rusche and Kircheimer, 1939; Melossi and Pavarani, 1981). Capitalist, state-intervention is seen as destructive and constricting in its ability to develop community-based programmes of crime prevention - as the state enjoys a monopoly over punitive regulation and behaviour in society. Social relations are thus described in the language of subordination. The autonomous natural creation of egalitarian and independent organizations is the political objective of these revisionist commentators. Such an ideological development is crucial to the control of crime through means that will promote class consciousness and working class organization (Brady, 1981, p. 185), for only the liberation of the dominated classes will lead to such a community wherein truly popular justice exists (de Sousa Santos, 1979, p. 264).

These two contrasting positions identify an ideological clarity between 'situationalists' and 'non-situationalists' which I will be using to advantage in the evaluation of this study. 'Situationalists', as the noun relates to crime prevention, base prevention primarily upon the geographical dimensions of a community or neighbourhood. The immediate environment of the neighbourhood is designed, managed and manipulated by them in a systematic and permanent way in order to reduce the opportunities for crime. In contrast, however, 'non-situationalists' take a less manipulative stance on prevention, concentrating more upon informal, integrative control based upon moral, rather than alienative, involvement.

The positions which have been described here are, however, ideal types and are merely theoretically based. They lack an empirical basis. In this respect a crucial element of the present study is the need to reconcile the empirical findings with these theoretical aspects. Furthermore, it may also be important to recognize the possibility that the limited intellectual impact of each of these contrasting and narrow ideologies has prevented intellectual progression to the notion of a dialectic relationship between the subjective and objective - between agency and power (Giddens, 1979, p. 6).

The scheme of the book

Data collected from selected research sites are presented throughout the book in the form of case studies. The evaluation proceeds through four, broad-based areas of investigation: residents' demand for private patrol is examined; the functional nature of the form of control is identified; an empirical and theoretical analysis is presented; policy implications are discussed and a new model is assembled which takes account of the extent of equity and freedom in neighbourhood private security patrol. Chapter 2 outlines research methods and problems. Chapter 3 provides a literature review, focusing upon particular claims and assumptions of opposing arguments in order to assist the analysis of the fieldwork. These opposing arguments are set against six key areas of research, each of which form a link into the equality and freedom debate. Chapters 4 to 7 contain the empirical data generated from the case studies. Finally, Chapter 8 summarizes the final conclusions, identifies implications for policy and introduces a new policing model which, in a modern capitalist society, can accommodate an increased level of equity of policing provision.

2 Research environments, methods and issues

Details of the research sites and the methods used are now described with a view to clarifying the objectives of a wider programme of research. The object is to outline the physical surroundings and circumstances of the case studies and describe the methods adopted for data collection and evaluation. First, profiles of the research sites are presented - less as explanatory and more as informational or impressionistic accounts, for the overall picture which they convey is important to conclusions made later in the study.

Case study environments

The research sites (case studies) were chosen on a purely personal basis. I was influenced in this by practicalities of distance and time - for I received no physical assistance in completing the fieldwork. I was also aware that the contrasting nature of variable environments could enhance the sociological value of the final analysis of the study. Accordingly, sites were consciously chosen to represent both privately owned housing and rented property in both urban and rural environments. None of the areas chosen had significant ethnic minority populations. Such populations would have complicated any straightforward class analysis undertaken because of, for example, social processes concerning 'scapegoating' (especially important in relation to residents' fear of crime) and the existence of high social mobility amongst ethnic minorities.

In addition to the three primary research locations which I describe below, I also visited the scenes of two other sites where private security was carrying out patrol in residential areas. Through postal means, I additionally sought to obtain information and opinions from other sources located throughout the country where I had been unable to visit personally.

Before proceeding with descriptions of the case study locations it will be useful to provide a brief discussion about case study method and its relevance to my research subject.

Case study as a relevant research method

Case study research is a legitimate research design in its own right and can be used to study a phenomenon systematically. Its purpose may be seen as twofold: to arrive at a comprehensive understanding of the groups under study and to develop general theoretical statements about regularities in social structure and process (Becker, 1968, p. 233). Thus, insight into how and why things are the way they are can be expected to result from this method (Stake, 1981, p. 47) and the knowledge which is obtained is likely to be more concrete, vivid and sensory than abstract. Resulting knowledge is also based more on reference populations (Stake, ibid., pp. 35-36). In this respect a case study looks at single instances with the objective of identifying their unique features. In contrast to purely statistical analysis, results are more likely to be immediately intelligible and have a three-dimensional reality which can be understood by a wider readership than the professional research circle.

A criticism of case study research is that the results, being so specific to an instance, are not easily generalised, except by intuitive judgement that the case is similar to another. The researcher's selectivity is not normally open to the checks which are made in large scale surveys. I intended my research design, therefore, to include several sources of evidence additional to my own observation. This allowed in objectivity and validity through measurement. These included interviews and examining documents and records. It seemed, thus, an easy decision for me to choose case study as a method here because it could encompass the use of many research methods and would also allow me to base the research around instances which I had already identified were at the centre of my considerations (Adelman, Jenkins and Kemis, 1983, p. 2).

It is important, however, that the researcher is sensitive to the biases inherent in case study research. Goetz and Le Compte (1984, p. 95) observe that it is one of the few modes of scientific study which admits into the research frame the subjective perceptions and biases of both the participants and the researcher. In addition to the need for sensitivity of such matters as the physical setting and those within it, there was, therefore, a need for me to ask how it could direct me to the next piece of data and how well it reflected what was happening. I found that the case study researcher also needs to be a good communicator and listener. A good communicator will empathize with respondents, establish rapport, ask good questions and listen intently (Guba and Lincoln, 1981, p. 140). A good notion for understanding the importance of this social talent in case study can be found in the anthropological concept of boundary spanning - which is defined as skill in communicating within and across cultural groups (Goetz and Le Compte, op. cit., p. 99).

Locations

Moston   Moston is a small residential street forming part of a large urban conurbation or 'new town' in the North East of England. It is a 'T' shaped cul-de-sac containing 31 high-standard housing units, predominantly bungalows. All are owner-occupied and they contrast with the area's more drab corporation-owned housing. Lawns and hedges are well trimmed, gardens are tidy and the appearance of the street and surroundings is particularly pleasant. Not one residence lets the other down in appearance. Properties are valued approximately between £100,000 and £200,000. The street has an air of privacy and isolation - a high wooden fence separates it from the Corporation housing at the rear - but there is access to and from the rented housing area by two public walkways. A public road gives access into and out of the street from a small open area of countryside. Within a radius of one mile there are several large industrial estates. Fifty yards from Moston, separated by grassed areas, is another cul-de-sac, similar in appearance and containing the same number of housing units. For the purposes of the research design its similarity to Moston is very relevant to comparative data analysis, especially the crime pattern analysis described in Chapter 7 relating to the notion of rational choice and crime displacement (Cornish and Clarke, 1986, 1988; Allatt, 1984a). Moston Security Services operate from a local corporation-owned house where the company's owner and his family reside. The company employ five mobile dog patrol officers whose primary work-area is the surrounding industrial estates.

Bridton   Bridton is a residential estate in a rural setting situated on the outskirts of a large town in the North East of England. To the north and east of the estate is open countryside and within a distance of five miles is the large urban conurbation of South Tyne-side. The estate consists of approximately 1,000 privately owned houses, bungalows and flats. The dwellings were built in two stages and finally completed in 1986. Property values are approximately between £50,000-£150,000. The patrolled and un-patrolled areas of the estate are naturally divided by a road. This factor, again, conveniently assisted the legitimacy of the comparative crime pattern analysis presented in Chapter 7 and its association with rational choice theory and crime displacement. The properties within the patrolled area of the estate are slightly more visibly attractive than those on the un-patrolled side. The overall environmental appearance of the patrolled side is similarly more attractive. These apparent differences, however, are sociologically insignificant as no substantial social, environmental or economic contrasts exist. The estate is bounded on two sides by council-owned housing and boundaries are well defined by large stretches of shrub-land. The estate's 'economic' separateness from the council-owned areas is immediately apparent. Brian, the private patrolman, wears a uniform he bought in an army surplus store. He most often patrols the estate between 6pm and 6am daily, either on foot with his Alsatian dog or in an estate-car. His reputation as a successful deterrent was well known on the estate while it was being built. Employed by the builders to secure material on the site, Brian had become popular by his sociable personality and ability to catch and deter thieves intent on stealing building materials.

Becton   Becton is a large London borough comprising an area of sixty square miles with a population of approximately 29,300 (Becton Council, 1991, p. 6). The Council has a progressive policy which espouses government ideology of effectiveness and efficiency through contracting-out of public services to the private sector (Ascher, 1987). The average house price is about £91,000 and 75 per cent of housing is owner-occupied (Becton Council, ibid., p. 2) . The Rams Estate, in the south east of the borough, comprises of approximately 1050 housing units. Types of dwelling vary and include blocks of flats, semi-detached houses and bungalows. There is a strikingly visible contrast between the flats and other housing in the area. Whereas houses and bungalows give the appearance of environmental normality the blocks of flats are typically untidy in appearance. Inside the flats is the smell of stale urine from the lift-wells and staircases. Graffiti covers both inside and outside walls. Most of the residents are young persons with families who are non-owner-occupiers. The Becton patrol, consisting of contract security personnel using four double-crewed vans, patrol the whole borough area from 6pm. to 1am. daily.

Data collection

It is now appropriate to consider the methods used in gathering data and some of the problems concerning its analysis. First it is necessary to briefly outline an important theoretical aspect which may impact upon analyses and, therefore, needs to be considered in the research design.

The analytic problem of modernity

Modernity (modern society) as defined by Giddens (1991, p. 15) has two dimensions, industrialism and capitalism, and it produces certain distinctive social forms, the most prominent of which is the nation-state. If one of the characteristics of the capitalist state in its most developed form is an increase in private security (South, 1988) then it is important in the present study to accurately analyse the processes which lead to this. This is not an easy matter for there are different ways of interpreting the nature of modern society.

There are two popular approaches to analysing modern society. The first, which gives emphasis to the 'controllers', sees society as an association of individuals who have conflicting ends and whose security and freedom will be ensured through the rule of law. This view is reflected strongly in neo-conservative social contract theory. The contrasting view of society is primarily a structuralist one and has a tendency towards Marxist or left-functionalist theory. It is specifically oriented towards the structure of dominant groups and classes whose true character is hidden rather than revealed. This view includes both elements of the 'controllers' and the 'controlled' - but whereas the first approach focuses somewhat upon consciousness the second disregards it. Both these approaches may be analysed as inherently ideological. Although I have used relational argument through the bipolar distinctions of the 'controllers' and the 'controlled' to assist in my analysis here, I am conscious of the purely analytical nature of this approach. As noted earlier, this device can have no basis in empiricism and is being used here merely to develop concepts useful to the study.

As alluded to earlier, there is an important need to be aware of the possibility of theoretical analyses which provide an ideological overkill. If the ideological imbalance is to be redressed the 'complex world of cultural sensibilities and meanings', not just the myopic dual analysis of the controlled and the controllers, needs to be part of the research design (Garland, 1990, p. 4). In the present study this requires an analytical interplay between belief and experience which will provide a conception of society based not just upon political and economic explanations but also upon social and cultural interpretations.

The public's perceptions of the object of study is, therefore, crucial to my conclusions. Accordingly, obtaining public views was important to the validity of the thesis and a considerable part of the research effort was directed towards that goal. An interview schedule was designed to reflect this aspect. Thus, I aim to show the social influence involved in the phenomenon of private security patrol. To successfully highlight this subjective factor may well illustrate that individuality is of prime importance to social and organizational change and that change may be explainable not only in terms of it being the product of coercive state influences. There is, however, little value in subscribing to a particular view of social reality which focuses upon the actor's definitions of the situation and then leaping to another level of explanation which can be typified as structural or lying outside the actor's own frame of reference. In this regard ethnographical data and official records were used as balancing factors where appropriate.

With interview data I have concentrated on a basic form of content analysis of the responses to specific questions with a view to understanding the quality as well as the distribution of types of response. So, as well as a tabular representation of responses I recorded respondent's verbal replies during interviews - for such merely numerical treatment of open ended data does not easily lend itself to sophisticated statistical analysis.

The sample

Because no personal assistance was available in completing interviews the sample size needed to reflect the time which I had available. Accordingly, I decided to interview the head of each household if he/she were present when I attended. I did not, however, adhere strictly to this as on several occasions I found the head of the household was unavailable. On these occasions I interviewed whoever was present at that time. On some occasions more than one member of the household was interviewed. I was able to visit each of the 31 housing units at Moston and only one householder refused to be interviewed. At Bridton and Becton, however, the total number of housing units was much larger, so I needed to select a representative sample of the total which would be manageable for purposes of time. This was done by the use of a computer programme designed to select random numbers. 50 housing units, estimated to be a manageable figure, were selected from the total population at each site. Each of the 50 selected householders at Bridton agreed to be interviewed.

After visiting each of the 50 units at Becton, however, the sample was finally reduced to 31 units due to the fact that the residents in the remaining 19 were unaware of the patrol's existence. As most questions related to respondent's knowledge of the private patrol I was unable to fully complete the interviews at these 19 locations although some data were collected.

I have attempted to confirm the truth of empirical analysis through the accumulation of varied data. The objective was to avoid a bland surface analysis of the quantitative data obtained and to interpret aspects essential for a deeper insight into the subject of study. Thus, although a considerable amount of the research programme included quantitative methods, opportunities existed for both structured and unstructured interactions between myself and respondents. In this respect I was able to confront residents in a natural setting while patrolling with security personnel. This allowed for a more meaningful response which identified how social actors' explanations and non-explanations gain acceptability in certain social orders (Becker, 1978; Edelman, 1964).

In view of this potential for unanticipated interactions an approach to the study was necessary to interpret the many and varied statements which would be made during encounters. The data obtained from all interviews, whether structured or unanticipated, was quantified using the method proposed by Oppenheim (1979) - after all the interviews were completed the responses to each question were noted individually and from these a coding frame was designed. This was studied at length and the highest frequency of responses were listed. These categorised responses were then numerically developed.

Researchers, however, must always bear the responsibility of their own involvement and ultimately accept that their interpretations of results derives from their own constructs. Accordingly, my interpretation of the data may well have set boundaries around proceedings. These boundaries were obviated to some degree by adopting a multi-method approach. The multi-method research design used here to attain the research objectives collected data through the use of content analysis of records of those providing the service and the police; content analysis of documents and media reports; interviews conducted with residents, private patrolmen and police officers; participant observation of police, private security patrols and residents during their daily activities, and introspection through my professional status.

The interview schedule

The interview schedule for residents and security personnel was designed in conjunction with the six key concepts identified in the literature review outlined in the next chapter. It must be said again at this stage that a review of the literature identifies a theoretical overkill in respect of left-functional analyses of private policing. Nevertheless, the object was to design a schedule which would draw out responses concerning the six key concepts but which would contain language to which respondents could easily relate. The wording of the residents' schedule was, therefore, aimed at inviting responses which would discover why they wanted enhanced security, how they perceived its main functions and effectiveness, and the extent of community feeling.

In total, 135 interviews were conducted with residents and 27 security personnel provided additional responses. The schedule for security personnel sought to invite responses on the quantity and quality of interagency co-operation. As a secondary consideration of design, and in line with classical procedures, 10 per cent of the sample frame were selected and a pilot questionnaire was administered. The pilot questionnaire did not lead to any change in the final research instrument.

A problem with interviewing as a method of research is that the subjective data it produces can be highly situational. For instance, during all interviews and observations I made no secret of the fact that I was a police officer. From personal experience this often invites antagonistic or favourable responses from those present, depending upon their attitude to the criminal justice system. In view of this I needed to be aware of any ulterior motives behind answers I was given, restrictions on spontaneous expression, desires to please me by responses favourable to my status as a police officer and other idiosyncratic and extraneous factors which may have influenced responses (Dean and Whyte, 1978, pp. 181-182). I attempted to minimize these aspects by explaining to interviewees that my research would not necessarily influence the improvement of their security and that their replies would be treat in confidence.

On meeting respondents for the first time I produced my police warrant card, introduced myself as 'Inspector McManus from Durham Police' doing some research about the private security patrol in the area and requested their assistance to answer some questions. At the beginning of the study I was aware of the possibility that the formal nature of this introduction may produce uneasiness in some individuals, for findings have been presented concerning the effect of the interviewer's authority and deference on the interviewee (Lenski and Leggett, 1960). There is, accordingly, an obvious need to avoid this effect. However, some writers have suggested that the interviewer should play the role best suited to the situation and this will produce rapport and co-operation (Cannell and Fowler, 1964; MacCoby and MacCoby, 1954). In contrast to it being a disadvantage, I found my declaration as a police officer created the opportunity for respondents to talk freely in a relaxed atmosphere about their general perceptions of security in the area.

Key concepts and data collection

How the data collection relates to the six key concepts used in this study is now briefly outlined.

Rationale for private patrol

At Moston and Bridton I reverted to the rather formal mechanism of visiting residents in their homes and interviewing them. However, at Becton, as the decision to hire the patrol was not a decision of individual residents but of council committees, individual residents were not interviewed regarding this question. It was, therefore, important that the research described as accurately as possible the decision making process of these committees. These council meetings had taken place four years prior to my research and this presented a potential problem of distortion in accounts. It was, thus, necessary to interview as many of the persons present in those meetings as possible so that their accounts could be compared for accuracy. In this way distortion could be identified and corrected (Dean and Whyte, op. cit., p. 185).

The ineffectiveness of public police to provide the level of protection demanded by the public has been a factor identified by some commentators. They claim that private patrols develop due to this impotency of the public agency (Marx and Archer, 1971; Sherman, op. cit.; Stewart, 1985; Albanese, op. cit.). In order to test the hypothesis that inadequate public police provision influenced the inception of private patrol respondents' views on this particular issue were taken during interview.

Community

The hypothesis that privatization is associated with community insularity and isolation, paranoia and prejudice (Suttles, 1972; Warren, 1969, 1977, 1978; Pitkin, 1981, p. 327) was investigated in this study - for the success of any policing strategy should be considered in light of the absence of these negative factors. But if community crime prevention is to be seen from such a macro perspective it is necessary to consider the patrol's existence within a wider concept of community - wider than the immediate locality of the neighbourhood receiving enhanced protection. Accordingly, the relationship between the patrol and the concept of community as an ideal was measured to identify the extent of social solidarity - not only in the immediate neighbourhood but also from a regional perspective. Interview data were used to analyse residents' feelings towards those considered outside their community. Additionally, observational data concerning the level of community solidarity in the immediate neighbourhood was brought in support of interview material.

To create a perception of the extent of growth of private security patrol in communities in England and Wales, and to identify the types of community in which it existed, a telephone survey of police forces was carried out. The headquarters crime prevention department in each police area was asked if private schemes operated in their area and, if they did, to describe the type of community in which it operated. The size of the private security sector is difficult to estimate (South, op. cit., pp. 23-25) and, accordingly, I did not find it an easy task obtaining accurate information on private patrol from police sources. On three occasions, having been told by the crime prevention department that no patrol operated, I later discovered information to the contrary from other sources. This was not due to any obstructive strategy by police - rather the crime prevention departments were merely unaware it existed, even though officers on the ground were aware.

Function

In addition to identifying the primary physical area of function I wanted to test the hypothesis that private security patrol allays the fear of crime (Donovan and Walsh, op. cit.). This would require collection and analysis of data from both physical and symbolic aspects. Thus, in addition to interviews, participant observation was used to obtain data over a period of one year. I endeavoured to become part of the patrol's work routine and spent approximately sixty four hours patrolling alongside security personnel and, additionally, spent long periods in conversation with them during non-patrol time. This method was necessary to allow the opportunity for a closer contact with both security personnel and their clients. A certain bond was created and I became accepted as a friend to individuals. Thereafter an atmosphere for easy conversation prevailed. This relaxed atmosphere, together with long periods of close association, meant there was ample time for discussion and debate. This opened up other research possibilities and generally assisted the overall enquiry.

Participation in patrol also enabled me to identify any function carried out by the patrol which I considered to be, or to have been, a function of the public police. Interviews with residents also sought to establish matters which they reported to the private patrol and not to the police. Contractual documents outlining work descriptions were also examined. The data collected by these methods were consolidated into a measurable form which were used to identify any similarity between public and private functions and the extent of co-operation between both agencies.

Surveillance

A fundamental question which required clarification concerned the primary control method used by the patrol. Evidence was sought to confirm the findings of much research indicating the use of preventative surveillance by the private security sector (Reiss, 1983, 1987; Sherman, op. cit.; Shearing and Stenning, 1982).

Crime prevention strategies which use surveillance as a primary method may have marginal effects in preventing crime yet increase the apprehension of innocent individuals (Klein and Luxenburg, op. cit.; Marx, 1989). There are obvious implications here for the interests of the wider community and not just those receiving enhanced protection. An objective of this part of the research was to ascertain the accuracy of the claims of these writers as they related to the cases studied. In terms of the pervasiveness of surveillance it was also important to identify claims from other research that security falls to all concerned, including clients (Shearing and Stenning, 1982, 1983, p. 488) and that security personnel supervise the performance of these non-specialised personnel (Shearing, Farnell and Stenning, 1980, p. 499). My participation in the patrol assisted greatly in determining the answers to these questions.

Co-operation

The claim by some that co-operation between public and private agencies widens the surveillance net, and is therefore detrimental to civil liberties, (Kinsey, Lea and Young, 1986, p. 122) and conversely that society gains by co-operation, (Sherman, op. cit.; Chaiken and Chaiken, op. cit.) was investigated here. To ascertain the accuracy of these claims a separate schedule was prepared and administered to public and private police personnel in an effort to establish the quality of their relationships. My presence during face to face encounters between the two agencies also assisted in drawing conclusions.

Crime control: indicators for assessing effectiveness

A review of the literature reveals no consensus on either the definition or the measurement of effectiveness (Abel, 1982; Lavrakas and Herz, 1982; Lavrakas and Bennett, 1985; Skogan and Maxfield, 1981; Tomasic and Feeley, 1982). Whether effectiveness is seen as the unlikely possibility of total elimination, or only deterrence, must be a relevant consideration. There is also a distinct possibility that police may be held responsible for objectives beyond their control - as the real nature of police-work is a debatable issue. Public police effectiveness is too often judged by the wrong criteria, which can be one dimensional and narrow. Thus effectiveness usually means effective in crime detection. The most fundamental purpose of policing - the maintenance of public tranquillity - is so vague as to defy satisfactory measurement. Quality of performance for an organization involved in social conflict is an equivocal notion, for one group's efficiency and effectiveness may be another group's oppression.

The reasons why individuals refrain from committing crime is in itself a complex matter and produces lively debate (Cornish and Clarke, 1986). But if one assumes that the sources of crime are primarily environmental, should effectiveness be measured in terms of decreases in environmental variables such as fear of crime, inadequate security consciousness, lack of a sense of community and poor relationships between private patrol personnel and the residents? Clearly, these factors should be considered in addition to simple crime pattern analysis. Accordingly, and as previously discussed, residents' perceptions of assurance and security as a measure of effectiveness was given particular emphasis in the research design. Residents' satisfaction with the patrol, perceptions of safety from crime and how effective the patrol allayed their fears, were measured primarily by their responses to certain questions in the schedule.

Three other matters were relevant to this part of the study and are now considered. They are contamination, comparative analysis and police statistics.

Contamination   How can the effects on community crime-rates be apportioned to one particular agency? An unsuspecting resident simply switching on the light in his home may affect the potential offender's rationality to further pursue his crime. Who, other than the offender, would ever know the effects of protective action taken by residents? Offender

27

rationality is an important consideration in this respect and can affect research findings. For instance, Allatt (1984a, p. 103) found her research contaminated through an unanticipated community policing initiative which introduced enhanced public police patrol into the research area. I remained constantly aware of this possible damaging factor and was relieved to discover no evidence of its presence at any of the research sites.

Comparative Analysis   Through a crime pattern analysis, using police statistics of recorded crime, comparisons were made of two similar areas within the research sites; one patrolled and the other un-patrolled. By this method an attempt was made to measure the effect that private patrol was having upon the rate of crime control in space. For if a particular area were secure the most likely displacement would be territorial - the contiguous areas with the same structure of opportunity, rather than to remote areas or ones nearby with a different composition (Reppetto, 1976, p. 175; Allatt, op. cit.; Cornish and Clarke, op. cit.). But what is the relevant social space for effectiveness? Does this relate only to a particular community or to the wider community? Is it effective to reduce crime in the patrolled neighbourhood but to increase it in an adjacent area through displacement? In this context displacement of crime is an important issue.

Police Statistics   Additional to the damaging effects on research from contamination, there are inherent problems in accepting the legitimacy of crime figures recorded by the police. In view of the fact that a significant aspect of the research method included the use of official crime statistics held by the police, it is appropriate to provide some discussion of the various extraneous matters that can influence crime reporting practices by the public and crime recording by the police.

Bottomley and Coleman (1980, p. 74, 1981) argue there are at least four different elements to consider when interpreting official crime statistics. Firstly, it is the public who discover and report most crime. Both Bottomley and Coleman (ibid.) and Mawby (1979) found, independently, that police discover only 14 per cent of recorded crime. Other studies have found similarly (Sellin and Wolfgang, 1964; Black, 1970, 1971). This means that the decision whether or not to report crime lies with the public. Secondly, victims and witnesses will report crime to the police in relation to their perceptions of police effectiveness and their accessibility (Tanner, 1970; Schnelle, Kirchner, McNees and Lawler, 1975). There has been considerable research showing that the 'dark figure' of unreported crime is a high one (West and Farrington, 1973; Belson, 1975; Sparks, Glenn and Dodd, 1977). In the present study an effort was made to identify unreported offences during interviews with respondents and the result was included in the final analysis. Thirdly, many crimes initially reported to the police will not end up recorded. Skolnick (1966, p. 164-181) found that about 20 per cent of crimes reported to the police did not find their way into official figures due to the way that some police force policy regarded some crime complaints as 'unfounded' or merely 'suspicious circumstances'. Other studies have concurred with this research (Lambert, 1970; Center and Smith, 1973; Seidman and Couzens, 1964; Conklin, 1975). Research in Britain indicates Skolnick's (op. cit.) estimation to be on the low side (Sparks, Glenn and Dodd, op. cit.). Finally, the way police decide to classify recordable crimes affects the pattern shown in official statistics - two variations occurring are the retention of originally classified crimes after subsequently being found to have alternative definitions and reports of prepayment meter thefts in dwellings being over-categorized as burglary.

Measuring prevention by the use of police statistics is, therefore, unlikely to be particularly accurate due to the matters outlined above. Where circumstances dictate the use of official statistics as the only criterion for purposes of evaluation it is, therefore, vital to take account of changes in reporting behaviour that might flow indirectly from the way that a community is policed and the police criteria for recording crime.

Statistical data indicated clearly that there were three main categories of crime at Moston and Bridton: burglary in a dwelling, thefts concerning motor vehicles and thefts unconnected with motor vehicles. The data extracted concerned only sufficient to ascertain what effects the patrol may had on deterring potential offenders from the location. There was no requirement for complicated detail of such matters as weekly and monthly variations of reported crime, modus operandi, point of entry or other particulars. The objective was to present the data in as simple a form as possible to allow a straightforward analysis. An annual evaluation was made which compared patrolled and un-patrolled areas over the period analysed. Rates for all crime in the police section area, wherein the patrolled and un-patrolled areas were located, were also consulted. These were used as a balancing factor for the comparative material.

Due to the relatively large geographical area of Becton and the number of patrol personnel who were expected to give protective cover, no useful conclusion could be made concerning the effect which the patrol may have had on the crime rate. A comparative analysis of crime at Becton was not, therefore, undertaken.

Exploring relationships

Private security patrols are occurring in many areas of Britain. This may indicate that the private security sector is moving closer to the traditional domain of the public police - a domain where police and public interaction should be at its greatest for efficient policing (Cumming, Cumming and Edell, 1965; Punch and Naylor, 1973; Comrie and Kings, 1975). And if the traditional roots of public police duties are being questioned, and private justice is beginning to blur traditional lines, then such phenomena are ripe for sociological enquiry. And such an enquiry requires more sophistication than just an empirical analysis of what private security patrol in neighbourhoods is and what it is doing. There is a need to explore its relationship to other social institutions like the Home Office, the public police and government - the state itself. This is necessary if any meaningful analysis is to be made about the 'privatisation of that security which all members of the commonweal quite naturally desire for themselves, their families, friends and communities' (South, op. cit., p. 3).

Of crucial importance to the final analysis of this study is the consideration of whether the empirical data generated by the methods described above can support the left functionalist interpretation of social order. To assist in that process the next chapter moves the study on into a focused interpretation of the six key concepts central to the equity and freedom debate on private policing.

3 The state and the market: contrasting views

In reviewing the work of writers on private policing six key concepts can be identified, namely: motivation, community, function, surveillance, co-operation and crime control. These six areas of debate, individually presented in this chapter, encompass the possible existence of two important contradictions of a democratic society - inequity in provision of service and exclusion of freedom. They are at the centre of the moral and ethical debate on the privatization of neighbourhood policing and their examination will assist in understanding the extent to which these contradictions are present in the empirical findings of the study.

Key concept - the problem of motive: freedom of choice versus economic crisis

If there is a clear move towards an increasingly corporate rather than welfare style of criminal justice provision the rationale for such change is not so clear. Among many explanations motivation has been seen as an historical process of re-privatization, (Spitzer And Scull, 1977a) a non-historical process of change from specialized to generalized provision, (Ascher, op. cit.) a vehicle for the diminishing of public expenditure (Minford, 1987) and minimal statism, (Thatcher, 1977) a vehicle for ostensible minimal statism, (Cohen, op. cit.) a means to offset the fiscal crisis of the capitalist state (O'Connor, op. cit.) and the result of ineffective public policing (Slynn, op. cit.; Albanese, op. cit.). Although varied, these explanations have two common concepts which run throughout each and which have important political, economic and social consequences. These two factors are self-help and public choice. Self-help and public choice are

31

especially important to the adherents of a neo-classicist/voluntaristic approach to crime-control for:

> Crime cannot be tackled by the police or central government alone. Your willingness to become involved with your community to make it a better place to live is crucial. (Thatcher, 1989, p. 34).

Self-help

For neo-conservatives the existing criminal justice system is basically just and practicable in its operation (Wilson, op. cit.) but a disparity is recognized between police responsibilities and resources. Citizens' efforts to control crime are seen as part of the public's growing understanding that formal control systems cannot effectively function without public support. This notion, that the public must primarily look to themselves for protection as well as becoming 'the eyes and ears of the police', is not only argued by the far-right in politics, (Adam Smith Institute, 1989) it also has added impetus as a central tenet of state policy (Home Office, 1984). An important addition to actual citizen participation in crime control is the private security sector. This sector is encouraged to provide policing services both by the far-right (Adam Smith Institute, 1991) and, perhaps more surprisingly, the state (Home Office, 1979).

Although public policing is considered by many as sovereign it is hardly so supreme a function in reality. Indeed, it is not a difficult transition from public to private policing provision - much public police activity is easily transferred to the private sector. This transferable area of activity has traditionally included 'soft' proactive based and non-crime related policing - similar to the style inherent in private agencies (Reiss, 1983, 1987) and therefore easy for private agencies to adopt. And further, it has been estimated that between 80-90 per cent of public-police-work is unrelated to crime control and law enforcement (Epstien, 1962; Misner, 1967). During the 1960's research showed that this proactive style was being increased by public police (Cumming, Cumming and Edell, op. cit.; Bayley and Mendelsohn, 1969). Reiss, (1983, 1987) however, suggests that post 1960's research can be interpreted as indicating a decrease in the 'service' oriented approach by the public sector. If this is correct it would be difficult to reconcile with recent official enthusiasm for community policing - save that an integral element of that policy aims at involving the public themselves, rather than the police, in proactive policing.

Moves away from pro-activity by the public police could be associated partly with the current economic and political climate which has brought with it increased rationalisation of the public policing function (Home Office, 1983) and a policy which encourages not only personal participation in crime control (Home Office, 1984) but which accedes to the use of paid security agents - the private security sector (Home Office, 1979). Thus the current Home Office strategy for crime control is dominated by self-help and interagency co-operation. This strategy emphasises that it is up to citizens to organize themselves in order to deal with local crime problems. So, although the 'service' or 'soft' end of policing provision was traditionally provided by public police, these aspects of policing are now part of what the Home Office regard as not fully the responsibility of the public sector:

> A primary objective of the police has always been the prevention of crime. However, since some of the factors affecting crime lie outside the control or direct influence of the police, crime prevention cannot be left to them alone. Every individual citizen and all those agencies whose policies and practices can influence the extent of crime should make their contribution. (Home Office, 1984, p. 1).

Preventing crime for neo-conservatives, therefore, is a task for the whole community. This principle of informal social control in crime control - the citizen, not the police as the primary agent of protection (Jacobs, op. cit.) - can be identified with a shift from offender based explanations of crime to strategies of community prevention (Roshier, op. cit.). Thus the self-help ethic inherent in this policy extends also to the use of the private security industry itself, for it clearly has the ability to influence the extent of crime. This de-structuring tendency may be seen by some as evidence that the modern state is loosening its grip on sovereign areas of the criminal justice system (Cohen, op. cit., p. 128).

Public choice

Freedom of choice in crime control is another crucial principle of neo-conservative policy. Whereas private choice is made by individuals on their own preferences public choice concerns collective action. It has a particular concern with the economics of public finance (Dunleavy and O'Leary, op. cit., p. 76) and looks more at bureaucratic structures than at the content of decisions made by those within them (Buchanan and Tullock, 1981, p. 82). In contrast to private goods, the provision of public goods differs in that the supplier may have an effective monopoly on provision and is therefore insulated from the consumer's dissatisfaction. Buchanan (1978, p. 17) encapsulates the essence of public choice theory thus:

In one sense, all of public choice or the economic theory of politics may be summarized as the 'discovery' or 'rediscovery' that people should be treated as rational utility-maximisers in all of their behavioural capacities. This central insight, in all of its elaboration, does not lead to the conclusion that all collective action, all government action, is necessarily undesirable. It leads, instead, to the conclusion that, because people will tend to maximise their own utilities, institutions must be designed so that individual behaviour will further the interests of the group, small or large, local or national. The challenge to us is one of constructing, or reconstructing, a political order that will channel the self-serving behaviour of participants towards the common good in a manner that comes as close as possible to that described for us by Adam Smith with respect to the economic order.

Accordingly, Hirschman (op. cit., pp. 313-314) argues that consumers can exert control in either of two ways; using 'exit', by quitting the form of provision or 'voice', by protesting grievances to the public supplier. However, neo-conservative public choice theory asserts preference of the 'exit' option over the 'voice' option (Dunleavy and O'Leary, op. cit., p. 121). The growth of private security as a marketable commodity (Spitzer, 1987) has given these alternative protection strategies to the public. The increasing level of advertising space given to the private security industry and the general availability of their services may well have increased the 'exit' option.

This public choice ethic applied to policing services encourages residents to privatize their streets to reduce crime (Elliott, 1989) and can be traced to neo-conservative ideology whose adherents favour a two-tiered police structure where:

> ...basic neighbourhood services are provided at a very local level while other services are integrated and provided regionally or locally........It would be open to each council to decide whether it should provide the local community force itself or under contract from the national or regional force or, possibly, in some areas under contract from a reputable and suitably qualified private security company. (Adam Smith Institute, 1989, p. 17).

The notion of individual freedom and self-help is, thus, important in respect of inter-agency co-operation - not just within Home Office policy but also within a conservative government's policy on crime control. Self-help in surveillance of the community is enthusiastically encouraged by this policy. And in respect of policing provision through the market, freedom is seen as the central tenet (Friedman, 1962, p. 14) and the natural right of each individual by virtue of his common humanity (George and Wilding, op. cit.).

From the more critical perspective, however, explanations for private agencies in crime control have a quite different motivation to the neo-classical approach.

Capitalist logic: economic vacuum - policing as an historical moment

Whereas public choice theorists explain state activities, such as the production of public goods, as the result of intentional rationality the capital logic school deduces the functional necessity of the state from the analysis of the imputed needs of capital (Dunleavy and O'Leary, op. cit., p. 256). In contrast to a voluntaristic concept of state relationships some critical commentators stress crises in social control which have their resolution in economic sources. The relationship between the law and the state is ideological - appearing to ensure legal equality but concealing its functions in reproducing a particular social order in which the form of the law has a hidden economic and coercive content (Carlen, 1976; Holloway and Picciotto, 1977; MacBarnet, 1982). The extreme version of this model is a consensually based control where citizens are seduced into conformity by the pleasures of capitalism (Huxley, 1932). In such a model of capitalist social formations state and law have objective factors and functions. These concern the type of social and economic relations which ensures the status quo of capitalist economic viability (Poulantzas, 1973). Thus we are required to understand legal structures as indirect expressions of middle-class interests (Tushnet, 1978, p. 96; Ignatieff, 1983, pp. 77-78). Crucial to this explanation is the notion that no matter how much one may try to penetrate the ideological smokescreen there is no way through it (Kafka, 1930).

This perspective requires an understanding that the fiscal crisis of the state occurs contemporaneously with increased corporate hegemony. Private affluence thrives on public squalor as state provision of some services diminish. The public sector is at the sharp end of reduced or stagnant resource allocation (Galbraith, 1969; Taylor, 1979). This explanation is posited upon the assumption that as capitalist society undergoes a number of crises the state seeks to obtain legitimation for its activities. It does this by enlisting the support of the private sector in the fight against crime - and in the surveillance of those who threaten the capitalist ideal of social conformity:

As it moves along its twisted course, capitalism requires an ever changing ensemble of strategies to meet new crises, and in the current period the 'remedy' is clearly based upon the 'privatization of profit' and the 'socialization of costs'. (Spitzer, 1983, p. 328).

Thus the form that policing takes is described as a creation of the type of capitalism prevailing at a given moment in history (Spitzer and Scull, 1977b). In this view the emergence of the 'new' police in 1829 was the result of the contradictions of poverty and wealth inherent at the time of the industrial revolution and the state's need to provide certainty of order. Policing, public or private, is therefore seen as an aspect of social, economic and political problems and occurs within a process of rationalization of social relations. The social organization of policing under capitalism will, accordingly, continue to be significantly shaped by state needs to contain the growing socialization of the costs of production:

> Thus we see that the restructuring of the state apparatus which is part of the general crisis of capitalism creates pressures to break through limits of the existing forms; yet at the same time, since it is through the state that increasingly the restructuring must take place, state forms themselves become the focus of struggle. (Picciotto, 1979, p.177).

Forms of policing which have emerged over the past two centuries are, therefore, seen as a reflection of, and a basis for, the progressive rationalization of social life in capitalist societies (Spitzer, 1981). Productivity in labour-intensive organizations, such as the public police, increases much slower than in its capital-intensive private counterpart. Thus, higher expenditure is required to keep the same levels of provision for public policing. And, consequently, unable to cope with increasing and complex demands on their services, the public police become unable to deliver the level of service demanded by some sections of society. Private policing in this view is logical for the perpetuation of capitalism as it more adequately answers the demands being made. The emergence and transformation of profit-orientated police services must, in this view, be understood as part of a larger movement toward the extension of capitalist control over the labour process and the rationalisation of productive activity.

Consensus and coercion have been seen as inevitable features of forms of policing and police-public relations. But such clarity of explanation rarely exists in reality - for various uncertainties exist at crucial transitional moments during these changes of form and relationship. Drawing strongly upon the theory that the domination of one class over others is achieved by a combination of political and ideological means, (Gramsci, 1971) Cohen, P. (1979) relocates the notion of consensus and coercion within specific historical relations and the situation of the working class of a particular area. For Cohen (ibid.) both consent and conflict are contingent, not inevitable, features of policing. The thesis he arrives at is about how wider socio-economic changes can fragment, unhinge and dislocate the intricate mechanisms and defences of working class urban society. An economic crisis exists in which a recomposition and relocation of the labour force is necessary. This has required a massive shake-out of labour and the resultant formation of 'the new lumpen' class. The political crisis is characterized by a tough law and order response to these dissenting individuals who are evaluated negatively by the media and the criminal justice system.

Using a similar analysis concerning the contemporary increase in paramilitary style policing Jefferson (1990) argues that the form policing takes has to be seen in association with a series of historical junctures, each of which can be characterized by either a high or low degree of moral authority (hegemony). At times of breakdown of moral authority (he argues that the period of 'Thatcherism' in the United Kingdom existed alongside a breakdown in moral authority) the traditional response by government is to grant more discretion to the police and provide tougher law in the interests of better order (Jefferson, op. cit. p. 136).

For critical commentators the arena for developing capitalism's productive forces has gradually become the sphere of human services such as health, education, welfare and crime control. And these are the very services which are most likely to be contracted away from the public sector as capitalism faces a fiscal crisis. Corporations, whether organizational or individual, are demanding highly rationalised, cost effective crime control. Police protection is insufficient for the needs of residents' interests and individuals will eventually look elsewhere for the expected services formerly rendered by the state. Therefore the private security industry receives a boost in personnel and earnings while the pressures on the public sector are relieved by private agencies' input into the criminal justice system (O'Connor, op. cit.).

But in its myopic description of economic determinism this theoretical approach tends to underestimate the autonomy of individual self-interest. Professions and other privileged groups in state and society may just as likely be responsible for the creation of policing systems (Berger, Berger, and Kellner, op. cit.; Ignatieff, op. cit.). Furthermore, contrary to the notion that the criminal justice sector has been starved of resources, there has been massive state expenditure on policing and many other public services have remained economically stable. In view of this there is a need in this study to allow in a social as well as an economic explanation of the motivation for private security patrols in neighbourhoods.

Key concept - community: exclusion versus inclusion

The longing for 'community' symbolizes a desire for security in our lives (Lee and Newby, 1983, p. 52). Its integration with the concept of 'crime prevention' must surely, therefore, be a powerful influence upon citizens and neighbourhoods. Accordingly, community as an ideal in crime prevention is in need of identification to ensure that comparisons can be made with the subsequent analysis of community found at research sites in this study.

Defining 'Community'

'Community crime prevention' may be seen as two strands which differ on many crucial issues. Importantly, these strands rest on different conceptions of what community is. Such differences concern, for example, what types of community should or should not receive most attention, (Kinsey, Lea and Young, op. cit.; Pease and Barr, 1990) the types of crime to be given priority for prevention in particular communities, or, in respect of 'minimal policing' of the community, whether reducing crime should be a priority at all (Kinsey, Lea and Young, (op. cit.). Differences of concern for the offender regarding intervention also exist and these too affect the definitive aspect of community.

These varied approaches to defining community within the context of community crime prevention are strongly influenced in their analyses by individual and group ideology. In this respect, while discussing the informalism of contemporary community crime control, Turk (1987) points to the rhetoric and reality of conventional thinking - whether it be from the political ideology of the left (liberation and communism) or the right (nostalgia and individualism):

Both kinds of rhetoric assume that people 'left alone' will naturally relate to each other in respectful and mutually beneficial ways. The considerable experiences and evidence to the contrary are discounted by alluding to the distorting effects of whatever presumptively alien, 'unnatural' forces (capitalism, socialism and so on) are blamed for 'dehumanizing' life. (Turk, ibid., p. 139).

Included in this analysis is the highly political nature of 'popular justice' inherent in the neoclassical model of crime prevention. Turk (op. cit., p. 140) argues that those involved in popular justice may be overestimating the receptiveness of the public to informalism and crime control. Like Cohen (1985) the concept of community for Turk (ibid.) is rich in the power of ideological symbolism. As such its political identity may be clear yet its true identity is unclear. It may merely be nothing more than a warmly persuasive word intended to benefit policy makers (Williams, 1976).

Thus, although the notion of community brings with it a general perception of high levels of social interaction within neighbourhoods, most research supports Turk's (ibid.) conclusion that there does not appear to be a common response to the spirit of community. If this is correct, an appropriate definition would need to take into account the likelihood of countless communities, each with its own micro-boundary. And there is much evidence to support this position. Those individuals who do participate in local groups, such as residents' associations, exhibit higher levels of informal social interaction than those who do not participate (Kasarda and Janowitz, 1974; Hunter, 1974). The propensity to participation is a middle-class phenomenon (Lavrakas et al, 1980; Skogan and Maxfield, op. cit.; Wandersman, Jakubs and Giamartino, 1981) and crime prevention strategies are more likely to develop in neighbourhoods with economic and moral homogeneity (Greenberg, Rohe and Williams, 1982). There is strong supportive research evidence to show that middle-class neighbourhoods feel more control over their environments and are more responsible for crime prevention by being less reliant on police than typical lower-class neighbourhoods (Boggs, 1971; Greenberg et al, op. cit.; Hackler, Ho and Urquhart-Ross, 1974; Taylor, Gottfredson and Brower, 1981; Taub, Taylor and Dunham, 1982). But these apparently successful efforts have their origins in self protection within parochial boundaries and, thus, may do little to compound any collective feelings towards community protection in the wider sense of the concept of community.

Active individualism and inactive collectivism

Feelings of 'community spirit', therefore, may well be reflected by the levels of community care in a neighbourhood for 'active individualism' and 'inactive collectivism' in modern communities is not an uncommon finding. Lavrakas and Herz (1982) investigated the reasons why citizens participate in community crime prevention strategies and noted the reactions of citizens to the threat of crime included: restricting their behaviour, creating physical and psychological barriers to potential offenders, and creating collective efforts with neighbours to prevent crime. However, these writers additionally found that most citizens who are aware of community involvement in crime prevention do not participate. 'Territorial attitude' and greater community involvement of active participants outweighed fear of crime and perceived risk of victimisation in motivating participation. Thus, research also supports the notion that only a small number of residents actually become integrated in community action.

The knowledge that community participation may be minimal, together with the general vagueness of the term community, further confuses the issue of definition. It is possible that there may be several broad meanings and yet the meaning of the term is still not exhausted (Willmott, 1987). Such vagueness can also be seen as resulting from community's dual nature of evaluative and empirically descriptive meanings - meanings which refer to aspects of society that are valued when they exist and desired in their absence (Minar and Greer, 1969, p. 81). Thus the concept of community can be so formal and abstract that, as a single entity, it defies social explanation. (Plant, 1978, p. 81). Some writers involved in the contemporary debate on crime prevention have recognized this doubtful possibility of identifying 'community' in general terms and see its use as involving an awareness of locating specific groups in specific environments who should be approached on their own terms (Hope and Shaw, op. cit., p. 26). In this sense, the quality of community may be described in a framework of social forces which contains ecological, cultural and political types (Burgess, 1925) or degree of formal exchange amongst neighbours' 'vertical' ties to the larger community and extent of attachment to the local community (Warren, 1969, 1977, 1978).

Three models of community crime prevention

When analysing the concept of community in context with prevention, Weiss (1987, p. 117), clearly and successfully develops a typology using three varieties of community, namely community as a locale for 'walling, watching and wariness, community as a mediating instrument in social service delivery and community as a cultural symbolic unit of collective identity (group solidarity). Rejecting the first two approaches as defective, Weiss argues that community prevention must be integrative and not exclusionary. Exclusionary definitions of community are in fact the very definitions which Hope and Shaw, (op. cit.) Burgess (ibid.) and Warren (1969, 1977, 1978) draw attention to. Situational crime prevention is, therefore, seen to be based on alienative ideology which creates a siege mentality - to the detriment of community and social solidarity. The first two approaches set out by Weiss are often associated with the neo-conservative ideology concerning private provision of social welfare (ibid. p. 13). In terms of the community concept, these strategies are segmental and non-integrative and cannot sustain 'community'. Community as an ideal should involve, thus, informal control through mutual dependence and collective responsibility.

Similarly, in defining the 'defended neighbourhood' in context with situational crime prevention, Suttles (op. cit., p. 57) alludes to small corporate areas with identities known by those within and without. Here people look for a good neighbourhood where it is possible to anticipate neighbours' intentions. In the process, distinctions are made between areas and, thus, boundaries are inevitably drawn. It is these boundaries which are dysfunctional to community (Suttles, ibid. p. 234). The defended neighbourhood, therefore, segregates people to avoid danger, insult and impairment of status claims. The quest for community can reach absurd proportions and finally become self-defeating. In this view, we should recognize this dysfunctional process and work towards its antithesis of a more integrative (Suttles, ibid. p. 268) and relational (Gusfield, 1975) definition of community.

For some critical analysts, however, all these attempts at locating the ideal community has an added dimension in terms of state repression.

Exclusion and fragmentation of groups and categories

For critical writers order maintenance actually requires community 'exclusion' (Cohen, op. cit., pp. 220-229) as a form of control:

> The vomiting-out mode stands for the possibility of separation, segregation, isolation, banishment, confinement......temporarily or permanently, deviants are driven beyond social boundaries or separated out into their own designated spaces. (Cohen, 1985, p. 219).

Here inclusion has led to exclusion by rehabilitation within the community. This 'fear of freedom' (Fromm, 1941) creates a situation where individuals want to be certain that there is a line of defence drawn between themselves and the psychopath or increased numbers of criminals living in the community. Hence the demand for 'order maintenance' and the increased demand for police patrol (Operational Policing Review, op. cit.). In this sense 'exclusion' operates on a macro level outside the bounded community (Warren, 1969, 1977, 1978).

According to this perspective not only persons in communities are involved in this process of exclusion, the state too has a role. Inclusion has led to exclusion through the development of government policy on privatization. Minimal statism has assisted in the introduction of private security patrol with its surveillance methods of exclusionary control. An inclusionary motive has therefore led to an exclusionary effect. The state, in this view, is seen as taking an active role in fragmenting society through inter-agency co-operation (Home Office, 1979, 1983). Public order will not be enhanced because inclusion and exclusion are mechanisms to increase the efficiency of the capitalist system and, thus, do not offer any solution to crime on the streets (Cohen, 1985, p. 234). And the 'private community' - the 'purified city' - is created alongside 'zones of neglect (Cohen, ibid. pp. 226-227). The fetishism of space begins as the better-off worry about their poorer neighbours stealing from them:

> With erosion of support for public institutions (school, welfare, police) and a decline of public services (whether garbage collection or health) the private sector not only offers replacement services (like private security) but 'commodifies' its own space. The pure market allows for increasing ecological separation based on life styles, age, special needs, degrees of deviance: buildings, blocks, neighbourhoods, even whole 'villages' which resemble medieval gated towns. (Cohen, ibid. p. 231).

One of the problems with this analysis is that it fails to recognize that crime is an intra-class phenomenon and that the majority of criminal offences do not take place in upper-class locations. Furthermore, such an ideology of economic determinism ignores a large area of human relations unaffected by economic considerations and able to create change of its own volition:

> ......the adoption of the penitentiary in particular and the institutional solution in general cannot be explained in terms of their supposed utility in manufacturing social division between the working class. This is because at bottom reformers, like most of their own class, understood deviance in irreducibly individual rather than collective terms; not ultimately as collective social disobedience, however much distress and collective alienation influenced individuals, but as a highly personal descent into sin and error. (Ignatieff, 1983, p. 92).

In conclusion, although community may be impossible to identify, its association with crime prevention for the purposes of the present study should appropriately contain elements of socially 'collective' and 'inclusionary' aspects (Warren, 1969, 1977, 1978; Suttles, op. cit.; Weiss, op. cit.).

Key concept - function: security for, or security of society?

In order to obtain a clear view of the functional nature of private security patrol it will be helpful to make some comparisons between it and the public agency. This will assist in drawing out the extent of egalitarianism which exists in the private agency.

Public and private police distinctions

Although private beat patrol predated public police patrols by centuries (Radzinowicz, op. cit.; South, 1987a) it is generally accepted that since 1829 the public police have had specific sovereignty on matters which require resolving by the legitimate use of force (Bittner, 1974). This reactive role of public police has been emphasised against the proactive role of the private police. Prior to the late nineteenth century, however, the public role of police was more inclined towards a proactive style. It has been suggested that the proactive means of inspection and observation adopted by private police may account for their growth in a market where the public police have failed to recognize the advantages of proactive means of control (Reiss, 1983, p. 91).

The main distinction between public and private police for Reiss (ibid.) can be made in terms of 'deterrence' and 'compliance' models respectively. However, many law enforcement agencies exhibit both elements of deterrence and compliance. The primary forms of law enforcement in compliance systems are 'inspection' and 'surveillance' while 'audits' and 'investigations' are more common to deterrence systems (Reiss, ibid., p. 94). The systematic use of the compliance style of law enforcement becomes possible when the goal of law enforcement in preventing consequences is too costly for the society to bear. It is also a dominant style when the public police function of detecting and sanctioning violators is so complex and protracted that they are regarded as inadequate (Reiss, ibid., pp. 94-95).

A condition which leads to compliance law enforcement is the need to control the likelihood of collective rather than individual harm where harm is substantial - even when the possibility of an occurrence is rare. Further conditions are the necessary protection of potential victims where preventable action can be taken and the need to intervene in systems to prevent harmful occurrences. An important aspect of compliance law enforcement is that it will exist where a distinct population of potential violators can be identified or events are predictable. Thus violations in compliance systems are often violations of standards that could lead to harms rather than actual harms themselves (Reiss, op. cit., p. 95). Although there may be distinctions evident between public and private law enforcement the concept of 'protection' of information, persons and property remains a common theme to both (Shearing, Farnell and Stenning, op. cit., p. 16; South, 1988).

Loss reduction and assets protection: a dominant function

The predominant function of private security is, therefore, crime prevention and the protection of assets. In this connection studies of more formal social control have normally concentrated on state-run systems and describe the state as having a monopoly on social control (Mathiesen, 1974; Cohen, op. cit.). Recently, however, a new debate on control has opened up which attempts to transcend this monopoly (Shearing and Stenning, 1981, 1982, 1983). Central to this new debate is the private security sector and the corporate ownership of property assets. There exists here the notion that environmental security is affected by socio-economic trends which in turn have affected patterns of access to, and protection of, property (South, 1987b, p. 149). Reflecting upon this change in a broader perspective some argue that new residential complexes displace the public and allow in private policing agencies:

A single public street....patrolled by the public police, is developed into a mass of private 'streets' (the corridors in an apartment building, or the walkways in a townhouse project) which in all probability will become the domain of private security. (Shearing and Stenning, 1981, p. 229).

The victims and the experts: buying and selling solutions

In contemporary capitalism many citizens are involved in a culture of consumption where buying and selling 'emotional security' is the norm, (Packard, 1967, p. 66) for citizens are demanding more protection of their private space than their predecessors (Reiss, 1987, p. 42). The culture of consumption has been traced to the rise of a social world which allows, for some, the resolving of crime problems and security by paying for policing services (Ewan and Ewan, 1982, p. 42; Spitzer, 1987, p. 54). Such a society has developed by the:

..............maturation of the national marketplace, including the establishment of national advertising; the emergence of a new stratum of professionals and managers, rooted in a web of complex new organizations (corporations, government, universities, professional associations, media, foundations, and others); and the rise of a new gospel of therapeutic release preached by a host of writers, publishers, ministers, social scientists, doctors, and the advertisers themselves. (Fox and Lears, 1983, p. xi).

Consumers concerned about crime thus have relevant emotional experiences which are responsive to the stimuli associated with the solution (Schwartz, 1973). This part of the self becomes the haunted repository of sensitivity, vulnerability, and emotion (Ewan and Ewan, op. cit., p. 262). It is up to the provider of the solution - the expert - to tap into that part of the individual which is responsive to the need for security (Spitzer, op. cit.).

Concern and fear: the psychological function

Property is an important physical aspect of private protection but it is also important to identify the emotional effects of insecurity. Any evaluation of enhanced security should not, therefore, only consider crime rates and other quantifiable data. Crime has several sides to its nature - victimization and protective behaviour are just two facets. A third and increasingly important aspect of crime is fear. Accordingly, the extent of 'feelings' of safety is a crucial ingredient of the policing function.

Studies in North America (Maxfield, 1984) and Britain (Hough and Mayhew, 1983) show that fear of crime can be as damaging to society as the acts themselves. Kelling et al (1974) and Allatt (1984b, p. 181) note how some crime prevention measures can have the effect of reducing fear whether or not they reduce crime itself. In the United States, Clemente and Kleinman (1977) and Katzman (1980) identified fear as an increasing and major threat to society and associated it with the decline of neighbourhoods. From a current European perspective, although Liege (1988, p. 254) concurs with this view in France there is little known about the effects of fear on society in Britain (Smith, 1986, p. 110). It is known, however, that burglary and street crime provoke the most fear (Hough and Mayhew, ibid.). In an age of advanced communications, where an apparent increase in all categories of crime is occurring, it is most likely that the fear of crime will increase. But what actually constitutes fear is debatable.

Defining 'fear'

Maxfield (op. cit. p. 3) describes the fear of crime as 'an emotional and physical response to a threat'. The primary defining factor has been similarly described as 'the emotional fear of physical harm' (Garofalo, 1981, p. 840). Garofalo (op. cit.) differentiates between 'physical harm', and 'property loss', the latter of which he describes in terms of worry rather than fear. However, he argues that if such loss is of great value to the individual then theft of his property is similar to a physical attack. In this respect offences of unlawful trespass to property to commit certain specified offences, by force or otherwise, may be considered as eliciting fear in anyone who anticipates victimization. Nevertheless, the precise character of fear has not been agreed upon, even though it has been investigated in detail (Baumer, 1978; Fowler, McCalla and Mangione, 1979; Garofalo, ibid.; Kerner, 1978). These writers would generally agree, however, that fear can be distinguished both from concern for crime as a local problem and from a general awareness of crime in the immediate environment.

Allaying fear by patrol

In his research of 226 resident patrols in American urban areas Yin (1977, p. 30) found that building patrols were effective in increasing resident's sense of security. Some further evidence has been found in North America and Britain that community crime control strategies contribute to decreasing the fear of crime (Newton, 1978; US Department of Justice, 1980; Allatt, 1984b). In the only known published research on private security patrol's effects upon residents' sense of security 88.80 per cent of residents found a positive effect (Donovan and Walsh, op. cit., p. 56). Primary functions in that research were found to be a 'visible presence' and 'knowing that someone was watching out' (ibid., pp. 58-59). The study concluded that private patrol was a major stabilizing influence upon the community (ibid., p. 80). From a critical position, however, it is the very un-stabilizing effects of fear on the community alluded to earlier that protection agents will take advantage of.

A belief system: the sinister function of securing society

Some critical writers argue that the public's dependence on the apparent professional knowledge of protection agents is strengthened through a belief system created by those agents. Similarly, the Home Office's crime prevention policy of inter-agency co-operation is an important part of that system and necessary for the continuance of panoptical surveillance. Unless, therefore, the panoptical structure is inculcated in a belief system it will not succeed:

> The view that there are good grounds for combating 'external and internal enemies of the state' is subtly inculcated. The belief that surveillance is not efficient and that we need more of it, is simultaneously disseminated and this definition of the situation also becomes real in its consequence. Both definitions of the situation are important for panopticism to thrive. (Mathiesen, 1987, p. 75).

Thus, state policy (Home Office, 1979, 1983) and general rhetoric on crime prevention and security is able to:

> ....provide the necessary belief context, the obedient, disciplined, subservient set of beliefs necessary for the surveillance systems to be functional. Concretely, surveillance in a broad sense, and certainly the policing of society, is given general legitimacy. (Mathiesen, 1987, pp. 74-75).

Belief systems, in this analysis, perpetuate and complement surveillance and panopticism, thus, publicity on inadequate police resources is necessary rhetoric for increased surveillance. The constant bombardment of our lives by the notion that we are being attacked from all sides and that we must protect ourselves has significant consequences for surveillance systems. As Nick Ross, presenter of BBC'S television programme Crime Watch UK puts it:

> Crimewatch has brought home to me that we can't just dismiss crime fighting as being the job of the police. We, the public, must form the front line. (Readers' Digest, 1987, p. 114).

The new professionals

So, for critical commentators the progressive discourse of crime prevention and the need for enhanced protection only strengthens the state's social control on communities. The state's accession to the development of the private security industry can be seen as part of this process. The neoclassical model of community management, within which the theory of freedom of choice lies, is being re-addressed by the Home Office (Hope and Shaw, op. cit.). New control agencies are being created by the state and

47

with them new professionals - private security personnel (Cohen, op. cit., Chapter 5). All this, for adherents of the dispersal of social control thesis, strengthens the state's control of the community.

Key concept - surveillance: intrusion versus extrusion

Surveillance, or 'Watching' as it applies to classical forms of crime control, has been defined as:

> ......the various methods of observing people and places that criminals might attack, as well as apprehending the criminal in the act if an attack does occur. It includes police patrolling, the work of private security guards, and voluntary citizen efforts, as well as the informal natural watching that people do when looking out of their windows and observing their neighbours. (Sherman, 1983, p. 146).

'Watching out' in this interpretation is perfectly legitimate and is encouraged by state agencies (Home Office, 1984). This aspect of the 'opportunity reduction' model and its application to private security patrols is derived from earlier theorising about how changes in physical design characteristics will reduce criminal opportunities (Jacobs, op. cit.). The perspective, derived through 'defensible space theory' (Newman, 1972) and 'crime prevention through environmental design', (Jeffery, 1971) argues that there must be increased surveillance in the community to reduce criminal opportunity. Alternative analyses, however, have a tendency to focus upon the sinister aspects of surveillance:

> We are becoming a 'maximum security' 'fish bowl' or 'surveillance society' where our actions are increasingly visible to outsiders whether we will this or not or even know about it or not. This has profound implications for crime control......and of course, privacy, liberty and community. (Marx, 1989, p. 517).

Intrusion and the penetration of society

Even in its most pure form - the prison - situational crime prevention may fail because inmates infringe rules. But, ironically for some writers, not only may situational prevention fail, it may threaten the civil liberties of those having the freedom of a non-custodial environment:

48

Beyond a certain point, increases in such measures as 'target hardening' and natural surveillance will have marginal effects in further reducing crime, yet markedly increase the apprehension of innocent citizens and restrict their free social space.......With crime prevention strategies, the deterrence of the potential individual offender through the certainty of detection by the police, aided by the flow of public information, is replaced by the opportunity for anyone to act in certain ways or to escape from public surveillance: obviously this raises questions concerning the interests and needs of the wider community, and not just the groups whose vulnerability to crime is being reduced by the measures. (Kinsey, Lea and Young, 1986, pp. 121-122).

Private security patrol here is seen as forming part of a contemporary shift from individual to collective social control:

But other conceivable measures may move fully away from individualism, and focus on control of whole groups and categories - through planned manipulation (with good intentions of establishing 'brakes on crime') of the everyday life conditions of these groups and categories. TV cameras on subway stations and in supermarkets, the development of advanced computer techniques in intelligence and surveillance, a general strengthening of the police, a general strengthening of the large privately-run security companies, as well as a whole range of other types of surveillance of whole categories of people - all of this is something we have begun to get, and begun to get used to. These forms do not represent a further development of the individualising prison form, but rather a certain break with it - just as the prison in its time broke with physical punishment. (Mathiesen, 1983, p. 139).

Thus, such commentators argue, we have entered a new epoch in the structure of social control (Cohen, op. cit., Chapter 2). There is a 'blurring' of the traditional boundaries of police and community. The community has been 'penetrated' by a carceral disciplinary form accelerated by aspects of policing being privatized. Community participation has become the vogue. The police have not only infiltrated the family (Donzelot, op. cit.) with subtle disciplinary forms of control they apply control at the cross-roads of all institutions in society (Foucault, 1979a).

This 'penetration' hypothesis argues that private security patrols blur the boundary between formal and informal policing and increases policing 'of' the community instead of 'for' the community. Mutual co-operation between public and private police will lead to a net increase in surveillance (Cohen, 1979) as private patrols become the eyes and the ears of the public police. This leads to an enhanced flow of information and increases public police activity. The opportunity reduction model thus increases rather than decreases the total number of offenders who get into the system. The social control 'net' is being widened:

> When matters such as boundary blurring, integration and community control take place, the result is that more people get involved in the 'control problem'. In order to weaken, by-pass or replace the formal apparatus, more rather than less attention has to be given to the deviance question. In order to include rather than exclude, a set of judgements have to be made which 'normalizes' intervention in a greater range of human life. The result is not just more controllers (whether professionals or ordinary citizens) but also an extension of those methods to wider and wider populations. The price paid by ordinary people is to become either active participants or passive receivers in the business of social control. (Cohen, 1985, p. 231).

This myopic obsession with surveillance as a sinister form of control is at the heart of the present research study. It is premised upon discipline as the key concept of the contemporary move from institutions into the community. Thus, the argument goes, disciplinary, carceral forms of surveillance are the kind which produce intrusiveness and threat to individual liberties. If, therefore, the empirical analysis of surveillance does not correlate with that of the 'blurring theorists' then their general analysis of 'community penetration' cannot be sustained here.

In view of the various analyses outlined above, the overall utility of surveillance in this study can only be evaluated accurately by examining the extent and nature of surveillance at research sites and the processes by which it obtains its objectives.

Key concept - co-operation versus confrontation

There are many private policing organizations, and hence private legal systems, existing within the community (Evan, 1962, p. 179) - these are, of course, additional to public policing agencies. If, however, the efforts of both public and private police are directed towards protective functions within the community it may be seen as illogical that they both appear quite separate in their organizational roles of protecting the public.

Models of public and private

For some writers the identification of separate agencies having many similar goals creates the possibility of an increase in inter-organizational relations resulting in either societal gain (Sherman, op. cit., p. 159; Chaiken and Chaiken, op. cit.) or loss (Kinsey, Lea and Young, op. cit.). Three of these models are now described.

The orthodox alliance   Some public police authorities in the United States have co-operated substantially with private security agencies to promote private patrol (Pancake, 1983). Because of the growth of private security and community crime prevention there is, indeed, a perceived need for public police management to consider improved liaison with private crime control agencies. To these ends some commentators have presented a conceptual framework to facilitate policy and operational decisions within the public policing system:

> For those involved in the administration of public law enforcement, it is necessary to develop policies that take into account the interaction of public police, private security, and community crime prevention. It is necessary for line officers to operate in a societal context that has fostered a set of values and attitudes towards these alternative crime control groups. (Henderson, 1987, p. 48).

This 'Exchange Approach' to inter-organizational relationships developed considerably from the 1960's (Levine and White, 1961; Reid, 1964; Aitken and Hage, 1964; Baker and O'Brien, 1971; Cook, 1977; Hall et al, 1977) and now dominates the literature from an orthodox perspective. Improved delivery of service to the public is frequently described as the main aim by these writers. A belief exists that inter-organizational relationships are significant for individuals, programmes and society as a whole (Cumming, 1968; Johnson, 1972, 1976; Hall et al, 1977; Savas, op. cit.). These beliefs and aims correlate to those of neo-conservatives.

Organizational power   In contrast to the orthodox perspective, the inter-agency co-ordinating and educative process role of the public police is seen by other writers as disallowing citizens to act independently of the police. As the state encourage public police to become involved in inter-agency schemes (Home Office, 1979, 1984) there will be a drift towards the colonisation style of co-operation between public police and other agencies wherein the former maintain a dominant role. The surveillance 'net' (Cohen, 1979, 1985) is thereby widened to the detriment of civil liberties (Kinsey, Lea and Young, op. cit., p. 122). This 'Power Dependency' approach (Schmidt and Kochan, 1972; Benson, 1975; Aldrick, 1976) sees the motivation to interact as irregular and forming only when the motivated party is powerful enough to force or induce the other to do so. Bargaining and conflict are natural forms of interaction since each organization seeks to attain its own goals at the expense of others (Schmidt and Kochan, 1977, p. 220).

Scanning for power   The 'Co-ordination and Conflict' model of organizational change argues that the degree of interdependence is an important indicator of organizational co-operation. Low interdependence leads to no co-operation in activities, moderate interdependence leads to co-operation while high interdependence leads to merger (Litwak and Hylton, 1962). From a left functionalist/structuralist position fiscal and logistic demands on police administrators will cause public agencies to 'scan' (Leifer and Delbecq, 1978) for alternatives to bolster lagging manpower during the state's crisis (O'Connor, op. cit.). One of the areas that public agencies can look to during the crisis is the private security industry (Boostrom and Henderson, 1983). Thus coercive state apparatus is strengthened through inter-agency co-operation (Mathiesen, op. cit.; Cohen, 1985).

Others express concern over the social control aspects of leaving crime control in the hands of private agencies (Spitzer and Scull 1977b; Marx, 1987; O'Malley, 1988). In the United States the intermingling of ties between private firms and public control agencies is seen by these writers as creating a vast information network supplementing the state's social control apparatus. There exists 'tiny theatres' of private control, (Reichman, 1987, p. 261). These sites of punishment (Foucault, op. cit.) exist in an economic and political atmosphere where governmental agencies and capitalist interests are increasingly dependant upon private agencies for protection. The primary source of protection is through enhanced surveillance (Shearing and Stenning, 1981, 1987a, 1987b).

Role conflict

Irrespective of ideological views, there are distinct practical differences between the two agencies which concern matters of structure, training and powers of arrest - differences which may create a barrier to co-operation. These areas of organizational incompatibility originate in role conflicts. At the centre of these conflicts are differing expectations and interpretations of

52

respective roles which create misperceptions, mutual negative stereotyping, distrust, status differentials, lack of co-operation, and competition (US Private Security Advisory Council, 1977, p. 4). To identify the extent of any inter-agency incompatibility must be a prime objective of the present study. Only when it is possible to view the incompatibility or otherwise of the two agencies can any ideological perspective be confirmed or denied.

Key concept - crime control

The notion of crime control descended from the nineteenth-century utilitarian philosophy of which Bentham and several others were proponents (Ignatieff, 1978, pp. 57-79). The theory assumes that human beings are rational creatures who are able to assess the costs and benefits of behaviour and will modify it accordingly, thus:

> ......the profit of the crime is the force which urges a man to delinquency: the pain of punishment is the force employed to restrain him from it. If the first of these is the greater, the crime will be committed: if the second, the crime will not be committed. (Zimring and Hawkins, 1973, p. 75).

Here public policy emphasises actions which increase the cost or pain of criminal behaviour in order to prevent the would-be offender. More recent debates, spawned by Bentham's philosophy, surround the massive growth of community crime prevention and its classical contemporaries - rational choice theory and situational crime prevention (Clarke, 1980; Cornish and Clarke, 1986, 1988).

Two directions for the crime control rationale exist, namely, 'deterrence' and 'target hardening'. Whereas deterrence focuses on the potential criminal and the prevention of criminal activities by threatening punishment, target hardening focuses on the would-be victim and the prevention of criminal activities by controlling opportunities for crime. The rationale is therefore split between a general and a specific deterrence.

Crime control and inequity

Although the neo-conservative approach to the management of crime declares that the inefficient provision of public services becomes a problem that the individual will resolve through economic freedom, (Gamble, 1981, p. 150) the notion of equality of mankind is effectively dismissed - apart from equality concerning civil and political rights. For to pursue egalitarianism is to deny freedom by imposing on society a preconceived economic and social system (Hayek, 1976, p. 87). Inequality generates innovation and subsequent efficiency which leads to equality. Thus, unlike classicism's problem of contradiction between formal and substantive equality, 'inequality' is admitted as a central tenet of neo-conservative ideology. It is because:

> ....we rarely know which of us knows best that we trust the independent and competitive efforts of many to induce the emergence of what we shall want when we see it. (Hayek, 1976, p. 29).

Thus the social can only be understood by individuals' actions as being the vital factor in social and economic well-being (Hayek, ibid. p. 6; Buchanan, op. cit.). Furthermore, the economic superiority of the western world is a result of individuals' uniqueness, responsibility and capacity to choose. This will lead to 'The Healthy Society' wherein:

> ....the vast majority of men and women are encouraged and helped to accept responsibility for themselves and their families, and to live their lives with a maximum of independence and self reliance. (Thatcher, 1977, p. 83).

The overemphasis on individuality in this creed has obvious implications for those who are less able than others to help themselves or those who merely take the option of non-action. Accordingly, for neo-conservatives the implications are positive while for others not so positive.

The ethics of crime displacement and the failure of surveillance

The neo-conservative crime-control message alleges that positive effects will inevitably and ultimately ensue for those who do not initially chose to enhance their protection. Realising their increased vulnerability through being without it, they purchase it and perpetuate the chain. In so doing, the 'common good' benefits. This is the theory of public choice in neo-conservatism and epitomized, thus:

> As a matter of fact, the very essence of security is that you will turn the criminal from the protected premises to the unprotected. (White, Regan, and Wholey, 1975, p. 40).

Another common criticism of situational crime prevention's techniques is that it 'papers-over' the problem and ignores its roots - treating symptoms and not causes. While the crime control strategy of enhanced surveillance may appear successful, when it is viewed from the purely local, individualistic position its apparent success is questioned. Research has shown how target hardening approaches temporarily reduce crime rates through displacing many incidents into unprotected neighbourhoods (Latessa and Allen, 1980; Allatt, 1984a; Latessa and Travis, 1986). The possible effects of displacement of crime is an ethical consideration which has political and social implications concerning the efficacy of the crime control strategy.

Although public choice theorists are apparently ethical in their outlook (any change which makes one person better off without damaging another is ethically neutral for them) (Pareto, 1966) their core value of freedom from the coercion of others has been shown, paradoxically, as restrictive of freedom (Dunleavy and O'Leary, op. cit. p. 93). Arrow, (1951, 1973) for instance, has shown that adherence to the Pareto principle (Pareto, ibid.) implies the dictatorship of at least one individual on many occasions. Thus, an economically advantaged individual has the ability to influence other less advantaged individuals by his action or in-action. Correspondingly, the idea of displacement of crime into the areas of others as a consequence of neo-conservative public choice principles of crime control, i.e. increased surveillance techniques equal displacement of crime, (Allatt, op. cit.; Cornish and Clarke, 1988) is likely also to be a contradiction of public choice theorists' core value of freedom (White Regan and Wholey, op. cit.).

Thus it is essential for any evaluation of the effectiveness of enhanced patrol on the distribution of crime to consider not only how it is affecting the quality of life of the recipient but how it may be affecting a wider public. Displacement of crime can occur, for example, where a thief is foiled by security measures at one target and seeks out another which is less well protected. In this way the major object of preventing crime is defeated. If crime is only moved from place to place, success in crime prevention must depend heavily upon how high a proportion of the total pool of possible targets can be equally well protected (Mayhew et al, 1976; Gladstone, 1980).

But for offenders the total pool of possible targets is immense. Target owners have various levels of protective need and of economic power. The importance of this variation in economic ability is very often neglected by those who argue for target-hardening. These differences create a moral dilemma for society. It seems reasonable to presume - contrary to neo-conservative principles - that those who cannot, or do not, choose to pay for extra protection should not be adversely affected by the efforts of those who choose to do so.

Displacement of crime and rational choice theory

Those who criticise situational crime prevention argue that reducing the opportunity for crime produces limited decreases and fails to lower crime overall. Prevention of crime is therefore not attained by measures taken - only 'displacement' to another time or place or some other type of crime is the result. In this view the main causes of crime are seen to be within the individual personality and therefore programmes to change criminal propensities will result in success. Target hardening is seen as pointless, for if the criminal wants to offend then whatever is put in his way will not stop him (Reppetto, 1974; Gabor, 1981). Such a position would tend to support the idea of 'displacement' for unless the offender's personality is changed, the level of crime he commits remains the same. If he is deterred at a particular point in time and space then he will only displace his intention to another target (Cornish and Clarke, 1986, 1988).

The belief in 'displacement' continues to underpin much lay and professional thinking about crime prevention policies and practices. Other commentators criticise the assumptions about criminal behaviour and argue that this assumption encourages the use of the term 'displacement' (Cornish and Clarke, 1986). These writers believe that the phenomenon of 'displacement' is better conceptualised in terms of a rational choice theory of criminal behaviour. Rational choice theory, although not synonymous with public choice theory - due to it being an elaborated theory of human action independent of any policy relevance - retains some comparability (Dunleavy and O' Leary, op. cit. 75) as it views the bulk of offending as the outcome of reasoned decisions about costs and benefits involved:

This 'rational choice' perspective on crime assumes that offenders seek to benefit themselves by their criminal behaviour: that this involves the making of decisions and choices, however rudimentary on occasions these choices might be; and that these processes, constrained as they are by time, the offender's cognitive abilities, and by the availability of relevant information, exhibit limited rather than normative rationality. Our own formulation of rational choice theory was founded on the additional premise that the decision processes and the actors taken into account are likely to vary greatly at the different stages of decision making and among different crimes. (Cornish and Clarke, op. cit. p. 933).

In this view, therefore, displacement is not inevitable and occurs only under particular conditions. The offender chooses specific crimes and commits them for specific reasons. His decision involves an appraisal process of different courses of action relative to its merit in achieving his purpose - a kind of cost benefit analysis. The attractiveness of targets to an offender by way of opportunity, rewards, and potential costs of detection is an example of 'choice structuring' (Cornish and Clarke, 1986, p. 935). These writers outline an impressive array of research supporting the concept of 'choice structuring properties' and suggest that certain properties may be listed, e.g. 'likely cash yield', 'risk of apprehension', which may be considered for the purposes of 'cost benefit'. 'Choice structuring' is thus designed as an analytical tool for understanding offenders' behaviour (Cornish and Clarke, ibid. p. 943). Selections are made:

> ....as being of most relevance to the task of comparing offenses and, hence, of establishing the likely limits of displacement within each offense grouping. Thus there is likely to be more displacement between particular theft offenses where they share similar profiles of choice structuring properties - for example, where the likely cash yield per crime is comparable, where similar skills and resources are required, and where the physical risks are the same. In contrast, where the profiles differ, this may clarify why displacement is unlikely to occur. (Cornish and Clarke, ibid. p. 941).

Further support for this conclusion comes from previous research showing enhanced surveillance as a primary factor in the considerations of offenders. When asked how they chose houses, burglars stressed 'absence of police', 'ease of access', 'inconspicuousness', 'isolated neighbourhood' and 'neighbours should not know each other' (Reppetto, op. cit., p. 16).

Although overall crime may appear to be reduced by target-hardening there may be considerable displacement which is largely confined in the local residential area (Allatt, op. cit., p. 110). This supports the notion that offenders are more likely to live locally, would be much more likely to know that enhanced security exists and do not move far from their domicile to commit crime (Normandeau, 1968, p. 263; Allatt, op. cit., p. 111; Maguire and Bennett, 1982, p. 82). Furthermore, actions, such as arrests or patrol strategies, constitutes 'deterring' forms of communication to locally based criminals (Kohfeld and Sprague, 1990).

Conclusion

The market is being used increasingly to provide security provision. The motivation for this development appears to have at least two possible rationale - at least two explanations of social order. On the one hand there is the notion that increasing freedom of choice will inevitably lead to improved security - not just for some but for all. On the other hand the degree of freedom for individuals to create social reality is limited by their economic power. Here, state structures are at the source of this apparent repression of freedom.

Thus explanations are either dominated by a social order of coercion or consent. Communities are similarly explainable - consent within, coercion without, inclusion or exclusion. Here the state's reasoning may be understood as either providing protection on a basis of blanket cover or merely for those with something worth protecting and in fear of its loss. Whatever the reasoning may be, the result either benefits security or invades its privacy.

And what is the degree to which the state participates in all this? How divorced is it from the mechanisms of private enterprise? Can the private be associated in any way whatsoever with state institutions like the Home Office and the public police? Answering such questions seems to depend upon whether the requisites of one or the other theory are met by the empirical evidence that will follow in the next chapters.

Penetrating the ideology

As well as having identified some primary debates in contemporary policing - as they apply to questions of public and private provision - the foregoing review demonstrates another important factor. It is that the resolving of the research questions being posed here requires an ability to balance competing ideological beliefs. In this respect, only if a methodological competence exists to analyse degrees of power can accurate conclusions be made. Whether moving towards a private system of neighbourhood patrol means a harsher and meaner system of justice or otherwise will only be truly addressed through adopting exemplary methods of investigation.

4 Motives

In this chapter the reasoning behind the demand for private patrol is addressed. In addition to the unstructured interview method for establishing this, the hypothesis that ineffective public policing was an influential motivator is specifically tested. Both an objective and subjective investigative approach was taken - data were produced from interviews with residents and others concerned with decisions, and official records were consulted.

The antecedents of private patrol

In contrast to subjective data, a more objective study is made in this section in order to balance out the findings. Antecedent descriptions of the case studies, and some other locations where private security patrols were operating, are presented. Social, economic and political factors which influenced residents' ideas are identified. Levels of pre-patrol crime and disorder and the effectiveness of police responses to them are briefly outlined.

Private bobbies, public beats

Evidence of the empirical existence of 'blurring' security provision in neighbourhoods was forthcoming in events purportedly occurring in the United Kingdom in the latter part of the 1980's. These events seemed to indicate that such a change in prerogative was happening. In 1989 some of the very streets and residential areas which Peel had filled with public officers were reported to have become the beats of private officers, paid by private clients. One newspaper talked of security firms 'taking over localised policing' on housing estates and investigated, in particular, four council estates in a south London borough where the council had contracted a private security firm to patrol the area (The Guardian, 1989, p. 27). I subsequently visited these estates and chose one - Becton - as a case study for my research. Becton is representative of the four housing estates mentioned in the newspaper article in question.

In another media report details were given of a suburban area of Birmingham where 97 per cent of tenants on housing estates voluntarily began paying an additional charge on their rents for private security patrol - security additional to that given by public police (Police Review, 1989c, pp. 740-741). The feeling that public order was being threatened appeared to be an important contributing factor in the reasoning for this demand for enhanced patrol. I visited the area of Birmingham mentioned in the report and spoke to residents, police and the private patrolmen. The area and housing estates were exclusively private and middle class. Public disorder and the crime rate there were no higher than in other areas of the West Midlands. It is also important to note that the entire land area where the patrol was operating has been privately owned by the aristocracy for centuries. Residents do not own the freehold of the land on which they live. The present landlords stringently control residents' freedom to change the environment on the estates. My enquiries ascertained it was the landlords who instigated the provision of the private security patrol and payment for its services was made by individual householders through an increase on their ground rent. No public housing estates in Birmingham were patrolled by similar strategies.

Private security's serious challenge to traditional public policing was soon recognized by the British Police (Operational Policing Review, op. cit.). Research carried out in twenty of the forty nine police force areas of England and Wales had indicated there were more than 500 non-police patrols operating in public places (Police Review, 1989a, p. 65). These private security patrols comprised an even distribution between those employed by local authorities on the one hand and those employed by business and resident groups on the other (Bailey and Lynn, 1989, p. 12). The Chairman of the Police Federation of England and Wales made clear the concern felt by British police about the introduction of private security into roles traditionally carried out by the public police. In a letter to the Home Secretary, he argued:

It is clear to me that this development involves an overlapping of the roles of police and private security to an extent which raises serious questions about public policy and the role of the Home Office.
(Police, 1989, pp. 3-12).

But attacks upon traditional services are not only specific to policing. The challenge to traditional policing is only part of a larger trend towards the privatization of public services in the United Kingdom (Ascher, op. cit.) and America (Savas, op. cit.).

Antecedent details of the three specific case study locations are now outlined.

The Moston Patrol   Prior to 1988 the residents of Moston had experienced very little crime in their neighbourhood. During that year, however, there was an increase of over 50 per cent on the 1987 figure. In addition to burglaries and thefts, minor street nuisances were occurring which were especially problematic to particular residents. Noisy youths from nearby estates, and others returning home from public houses, disturbed the residents in the street by using it as a short-cut home. There was a reluctance by some residents to venture outside in the late evening (Lavrakas and Herz, op. cit.). Youths playing on grassed areas and climbing trees in the street were another source of complaint. A group, who continually kicked a football against a nearby 'bus shelter until the early hours of the morning, was especially troublesome to some families at one end of the street. These problems had continued for a number of months prior to and during 1988. Some residents had complained to local police in the hope that these nuisances could be eliminated - but the problems continued. The residents' description of the disorder problems in their street portrayed an annoyance and exasperation in community members which was not being quelled by police action. In some instances a divergence was apparent between what residents and police perceived as priority policing. There were no indications that the police were using their discretion concerning whether or not they attended to minor complaints at Moston.

A Neighbourhood Watch scheme existed at Moston but residents told me that it was ineffective and that the scheme existed in name only. During my interactions with the residents and police at Moston I saw no evidence of the Neighbourhood Watch Scheme in action. One resident was still identified as the liaison person between the police and other residents but there were no regular meetings or any other organizational events that could be associated with a working scheme. Worst of all for residents was the fact that they could not identify any police officer who had particular responsibility for their area. This had not always been the case. In the past there had been a close and effective liaison between a particular community policeman and residents. However, the regularity and effectiveness of this liaison had diminished after the officer had transferred to another area. Residents still spoke of this officer in an approving manner.

The county police force was apparently experiencing a manpower crisis. The Chief Constable told a local newspaper that although it had gained 203 officers in 1986 the force was still 615 officers under strength. On average, an officer in the force dealt with forty four crimes per year compared with a national average of thirty five. Having seen that the Neighbourhood Watch scheme was ineffective there was a general feeling by residents at Moston that police were now powerless to resolve their crime and disorder problems. Residents' perception of police as an impotent agency of order and crime deterrence, together with the spate of crimes and nuisance occurring in 1988, led them to consider what other measures could be implemented to prevent crime (Boggs, 1971; Taub, Taylor and Dunham, op. cit.; Greenberg, Rohe, and Williams, 1985).

Hiring the private patrol at Moston was a consensus decision on behalf of residents (Lavrakas and Herz, op. cit.). Three residents, who were particularly concerned about the rise in local crime, (Kasarda and Janowitz, op. cit.; Hunter, op. cit.) first canvassed others on their feelings and attitudes and solid agreement to take action to obtain extra protection was found. The enthusiasm of the three 'prime-movers' in the scheme of action was vital. It is unlikely that Moston Security Services would have been approached at all had it not been for these three residents. Importantly, an 'exit' option was being taken (Hirschman, op. cit.) which gave a boost in personnel and earnings to the private security sector while simultaneously relieving a hard-pressed public policing system (O'Connor, op. cit.).

It is illustrative of the growth of security as a marketable commodity (Spitzer, 1987) that one of the three 'prime mover' residents telephoned Moston Security Services after seeing an advertisement in a local newspaper offering patrol services. Moston Security Services did not normally patrol in residential areas and had not done so on any previous occasions. In view of this the owner of the security company was invited to a meeting with residents to discuss the viability of the scheme and after a detailed discussion he undertook to provide the service. He emphasised it was important that all residents supported the scheme - a patrol which would operate for services of only half the residents would inevitably be giving a 'free ride' to those who did not pay. This creates the assumption that, unless a majority of residents in any neighbourhood become part of the collective action, security services are unlikely to provide a service which will benefit 'free riders'. Indeed, the owner of the security company at Moston had been approached by residents from an area adjacent to Moston and asked if he would be willing to provide a similar service there. The owner refused, having first surveyed the residents and found that although a majority of them wanted the service this did not amount to 100 per cent of the residents.

In a large group, where actors' dissent to collectivism may go un-sanctioned and they stand to gain equally from the group's success, collective action can be hard to attain because each actor knows that whether or not collective benefits will be secured the outcome will not be influenced by his personal contribution (Olson, 1965). Thus, collective organizations exist because they can control 'selective incentives' - which relate to private rather than public goods. These incentives are denied to members outside the collectivity. This collective aspect of community - apparently consensual and idyllic - is rather conducive to the 'segregated', 'defended neighbourhood' (Suttles, op. cit.).

The Bridton patrol   In 1986, when the Bridton Housing Estate was being extended, the builders subcontracted a security company to protect assets on the site. The patrol consisted of one security guard - Brian. He was an extremely enthusiastic patrolman and his success in protecting materials on the site had created for him a reputation of efficiency and reliability. Brian was, thus, respected by employer, local residents and police alike. His dogged patrolling style had resulted in a number of arrests of offenders found stealing materials. He was also very popular due to his open and friendly personality. By the time of completion of the building work Brian had consolidated his position of trust, respect and popularity in the community. The local police sergeant confirmed Brian's reputation and the fact that the local community desired his services because he had made a good job of taking care of their homes when under construction. They wanted Brian to continue looking after their security after their homes were built.

At the time work on the Bridton estate was almost completed a spate of offences to property occurred over a continuous two month period. The most worrying of these for residents were daytime burglaries. It was apparent that the crime rate on the potentially patrolled area of the estate was disproportionate to the rate on the area unpatrolled. From my examination of police records it became obvious that the dominant problem at Bridton consisted of property crime. Interviews with residents confirmed this finding. A search of police records and interviews with residents failed to trace any significant problem of nuisance or disorder.

Simultaneously with residents' concern about the rise in crime on the estate Brian's employment was terminated due to completion of the building work. Thereafter it appeared - from the informal discussions between some residents and Brian - that the idea emerged of a private patrol as a response to the emotional and physical threat which existed in the community (Maxfield, op. cit., p. 3). Two particular individuals were especially active in promotion of the idea (Kasarda and Janowitz, op. cit.; Hunter, op. cit.). From interviews with these two persons it became apparent that they placed great importance on crime prevention. One of these 'prime movers' described to me the period before the patrol's inception:

> There were several break-ins. Me and Brian were friendly and often had a chat as he patrolled about. He's very reliable. I told him I thought it was a good idea if he began doing the patrol. It was my idea. I'm very security conscious. He said he would try and I wrote a letter to introduce him to the neighbours. He went to their doors and the patrol eventually began.

The second resident explained:

> Brian used to check the compound opposite our house. He kept an eye on our houses as well. I talked to Brian after the break-ins started and suggested that he take this job on. He said he was interested. He went around the neighbours asking if they were interested. Then he started the patrol.

These 'active' individuals, like those at Moston, exhibited qualities of leadership and authority which assisted in the installation of a new agency that would avoid the inefficient bureaucratic public form (Seligman, 1973, p. 354).

After canvassing residents in 1986 Brian had obtained approximately 200 clients. He made a charge of £1.00 per household per week for his service. Due to a reduction in client numbers, this charge subsequently rose to £1.50. Having spent a considerable period of time accompanying the Bridton patrol I found that Brian constantly complained about the 'free ride' non-paying residents received from his service (Olson, op. cit.).

The Becton patrol Throughout the 1980's Becton Borough Council began to outline a new, future style of management to be practised by the council's officers. This style was predicated upon a 'generalized' rather than a 'specialized' form of provision (Ascher, op. cit.). Managers were reminded of the need for continuing change towards a management approach which would be better equipped to deal with the current climate in local government (Becton Council, 1989). A shift in management style had occurred in response to economic pressures over recent decades. This shift was specifically spelled out by the Council (Becton Council, op. cit., p. 6).

The change in management style had emanated from a 1983 publication by the Audit Commission for Local Authorities in England and Wales on economy, efficiency and effectiveness (Audit Commission, 1983; Minford, op. cit.). The management policy of council housing is seen by the Audit Commission as particularly important - local authorities manage five million dwellings in England and Wales, one third of the country's housing stock, and worth about £100 billion. Housing is the most important activity of most district councils, and the local government service that provokes the greatest volume of public complaints. The efficiency of services provided by public housing departments, and the fiscal accountability with which it was to proceed, was emphasised in the Audit Commission documents. Co-operation of council managers in the implementation of the policy would be required for successful provision of services (Audit Commission, 1984, p.15). Thus for the Chief Officer of Becton Council, the message from the Commission was clear:

Collectively it adds up to a reform programme based on 'free market' principles which are a long way from the structures, policies and sentiments shared for so long by members and officers. The need to separate the operations of client and contractor; the commercialism that will follow in the wake of setting up of direct service organisations; and the importance of customer/end user satisfaction cannot fail to affect the future. (Becton Council, 1989, p. 7).

Thus, customer satisfaction via the free market (Friedman, op. cit.) was high on Becton Council's list of objectives - service users were to be given maximum attention (Becton Council, ibid., p. 9).

In the four housing objectives listed by Becton in their strategy statement for 1991 their commitment to providing improved environmental quality for tenants was apparent. It was in this culture of effectiveness and efficiency towards an improved public service that the possible use of a private security patrol was to be suggested at a Housing Committee meeting in November, 1984. Central to the new strategy was competitive tendering and 6 security firms were invited to submit tenders. The ideological nature of competitive tendering is evident in other research where administrators took on the initiative of privatization as a 'crusade' (Ascher, op. cit., p. 264).

Subjective Views

For this part of the study two questions were designed into the interview schedule - one on motives generally and the other on police effectiveness. At Moston and Bridton both these questions were put to individual residents. Council tenants at Becton, however, were not individually questioned on the matter of motives as their views on private patrol had been represented by the Federation of Becton Council Tenants. The Federation had made the decision to hire the patrol with council executives in committee. Unfortunately, no detailed records of policy decisions on this matter were kept by the council. In order, therefore, to identify the reasoning behind the Becton decision it was necessary to seek the individual views of members of the representative body and the council. However, the question on police effectiveness was included in the schedule for the Becton sample and was put individually to Becton residents. Data from the questionnaire at all sites and, additionally, from Becton Council officials and the Federation of Becton Council Tenants, is now outlined.

Moston and Bridton

Most respondents at Moston and Bridton expressed anxiety for continuing increases in local crime and disorder and the fear of personal victimization. A significant percentage of those surveyed at each site stated that inadequate police protection was their primary motivator. 26.7 per cent of Moston residents and 33.9 per cent of Bridton residents saw inadequate police protection as the primary motivator for hiring the patrol. A larger proportion, however, - 73.3 per cent of Moston residents and 66.1 per cent of Bridton residents - saw the primary motivator as a concern or fear for victimization due to increased local crime and disorder.

At a time when residents were experiencing more crime and police were having more reported to them, residents were realistic about how much preventative patrol and security and assurance the police could give in the present climate of fiscal management. Although they understood that the police organization was currently unable to satisfy these necessities adequately, residents' still believed that responsibility for this provision rested with the public police.

At Becton the following responses were typical of those persons closely concerned with council policy on the implementation of patrol. The principal officer in charge of the research department saw the reasoning as relating mainly to the increasing problems of crime and disorder on estates and the inability of the police to affect any change in that situation:

It began after we received a committee report on unsafe housing estates. We asked why police and caretakers were not keeping the estates safe. There had been some victimization of caretakers after they had tried to sort out some problems. They were only there to clean really. There was a lot of vandalism by kids. Residents said 'Why not tackle the police about it?' We had a meeting with the police. The residents were concerned about some things that the police said they had no power to deal with - loitering and other things. The police said they were unable to help on those sorts of things. Someone came up with the bright idea of having a private security patrol to move kids on, stop violence and put tenant's minds at rest. The council had to show that something was being done. The patrol was brought about in this way. The Tenants' Association wanted it and the council wanted to provide something. We put together a pilot scheme.

The Federation of Becton Council Tenants, had an important effect on overall decisions to hire private security. The lack of police manpower to deal with minor nuisance was also seen by them as a contributing factor. A senior Federation representative told me:

The Federation started in the 1960's. At first the Council saw us all as anarchists and reds. It was only in 1970 that the Council took us seriously. In the 1980's, from the tenants side, we were on about the petty problems on estates, rather than any crime problems. We brought this up at the committee meetings over the years and eventually private security patrols came up. The Housing Committee discussed it every six weeks for about a six month period. Ideas were sent to the Tenants Liaison Committee. We thought it was a good idea. There were a number of councillors who were totally against the idea. The Police at Becton were having manpower difficulties. We asked the council if they would contact a private security firm. It was a good chance for the tenants.

A hyperbola: ideological motive

From my interviews with Becton Council employees, and other personnel involved with the instigation of the private patrol, the political and ideological nature of the council's policy-stance became apparent. In contrast to a description of the patrol's inception as a process of non-political and democratic decision making, a contrary perception tended to emerge. Interviews with senior council officials conveyed to me a picture of a council whose policy of competitive tendering would be implemented at all costs. Not only had this policy to work in practical terms, it had to be also 'seen' to be working. A council policy officer, who had worked on the introduction of the patrol pilot scheme, saw the decision as strongly political:

> Becton sees itself as a paternalistic Tory borough providing the service it sees fit. The private security patrol was a public relations exercise which gave hype to its political decisions on privatizing services.

A council research officer confirmed the council's intransigence to disband the patrol and allocate the money saved to other methods of estate security - methods more fundamental to specifically vulnerable groups but not so committed to government policy:

> I suggested that the money the Council were spending on security patrols could be better spent on certain groups such as the elderly or women living alone - improved lighting and other ideas to assist those groups who badly need security. I was laughed out of the office.

This person ceased employment with Becton Council during the period of my research. I was told by other employees that the officer's political ideas on the allocation of resources did not rest comfortably with the ideas of the council hierarchy. A senior research officer, previously employed by the council at the inception of the patrol, and whose research had been instrumental in council decisions to contract the private company, described personal reservations about the project:

> You have to remember that Becton has to be seen as a forward looking council and be seen as caring. The residents had never heard of private security patrols. The idea came about through council officers' application to policy. It would not be fair to say that it was the residents clamouring for private patrols - they weren't even asked, and it was debatable whether the Tenants' Federation opinions were representative of their feelings. They were meant as a deterrent but they were really a 'sop' by Becton Council.

With regard to some of the above statements it is appropriate to note that there are difficulties in interpreting informants' reports of data which they recollect from the past. Respondents have a tendency to modify past feelings so that they fit more comfortably into their current point of view (Dean and Whyte, op. cit., p. 181). This may result in simple omission, addition or distortion. The reliability of this ex-employee data may, therefore, be questionable in the light of the possibility of 'biographical reconstruction' (Schutz, 1962). However, the comparison between the interpretations given by these two ex-employees and the others does not show much variation and must, accordingly, be seen as corroborated (Dean and Whyte, op. cit., p. 185).

Thus, although Becton Council's common objective was apparently visible, it seemed that certain groups were not allowed full access to the power-base of the policy machinery (Kafka, op. cit.). A member of the Tenants' Federation also alluded to the Council's tendency to preclude members of the Federation from decision making:

> I'm suspicious of the Council. We appear suspicious to them too. They don't allow us to get involved in early negotiations. They say we will have no useful input, but tenants' views should be available at all stages. They say we may leak information. We asked to have the Council's 'One Per Desk'(OPD) computer in our premises for basic information such as telephone numbers etc., so we could contact people quickly. They said no, we may misuse information. Yet another group who have the computer recently leaked the council's policy of selling off council property to the private sector. It's a con. I have seen manipulation by the architects and housing officers at the Council. The architects develop an idea together with residents but when the design stage arrives they have produced something quite different. When we tell them they say, 'It's too late now'.

A senior officer in the housing department supported the above view. The description given by this officer was one of impotent Federation members, not wholly representative of the tenants and who aligned themselves meekly with manipulative council decision-makers on committees:

> The residents don't protest. You can tell them that they have to pay some increase or they are not going to get some improvement. They do not protest. They are so used to the cutback policy. I feel like saying, 'Say something, for goodness sake!' The Residents' Association members are so dependent on the council that they do not protest either. I've seen council officers feed ideas to the Residents' Association and they have taken them up later and developed them into policy. The Residents' Association is manipulated by some officers.

The balance of power, apparently lying with the council and the better-off tenants (75 per cent owner-occupation), reminded me that the sociological writing of some of those who criticise the conventional approach to crime control is of the type which tries to make the world look different. Here there is a gap between our private sense of what is going on around us and the professional discussions and writings of the social world (Gramsci, op. cit., p. 210). The argument goes that the state may be more concerned with the finer points of political economy than with those persons caught up in the victimization process - an overbearingly coercive and divisive apparatus exists at the centre of which is an economic logic. But it must be argued that this theory of conspiracy was hardly tenable at Becton for tenants were strongly influencing their own future. Furthermore, it is an exaggeration which undermines individual intelligence to argue such human passivity (Thompson, 1975, pp. 62-263).

A more appropriate analysis here is one which rejects the tendency to romanticise crime and see it as politically inspired. This left-realist position retains theoretical ideas and political ideals of the left but at the same time it accepts that crime does real harm. A radical victimology is called for by those who take this position. At the centre of this approach is a realistic and empirically informed picture of the extent of crime (particularly crime within the working class) and the extent to which some sections of society fear crime (Young, 1986, pp. 17-21).

Impotent Police

To further test the hypothesis that inadequate police protection had been influential in respondents' decisions to hire private patrol they were asked if they believed police could adequately protect their interests. On average, 97 per cent of respondents believed that police were unable to do this.

An important difference between the responses from Moston/Bridton and Becton was apparent. The Becton respondents did not appear to be as uncertain about police ability to provide protection as those at Moston and Bridton. This is a significant finding when it is considered that the private initiative at Becton did not primarily originate from local people but from New Right ideologies in Becton Council.

The Assistant Director of a Metropolitan Borough Council in the North of England, in his reply to my enquiry on why his council had adopted private security patrol, supported the findings at research sites. He told me:

It remains a central concern of my Council, however, that the Police are unable to protect public property to this extent and appear almost disinterested in incidents of theft and vandalism that are reported to them.

The perceived inability of the police to effectively perform their tasks was thus found to be a significant factor in the introduction of private security patrol (Slynn, op. cit., Albanese, op. cit., p. 86).

A demand for order

During interviews at all sites I found a considerable number of individuals spoke of an apparent bygone age of 'police administered order'. Many felt the police were more effective when they gave justice on the spot - as they had apparently been more inclined to do in the past. There was consistent nostalgic recall from respondents of the policeman who controlled community order. A typical example of this came from a middle-aged Bridton resident who recalled that the local policeman would, 'clip your ear and send you on your way. When you got home you didn't dare tell your parents 'cause you'd get another clip'.

The stories I was being told by respondents about their younger days often included some form of mild violence by the local policeman - usually a clip with a glove or a lash with a cape. The regularity of these descriptions given by interviewees portrayed a past era where the local policeman's distribution of discipline was embedded in society (Foucault, op. cit.). Now, however, there was a substantial feeling of sorrow amongst respondents for what can only be described as a loss of discipline in the community. 60 per cent saw its immediate return as an important need which could be realized to some extent by the return of the policeman on the beat.

This data has been compared with attitude data from other research samples to try and establish whether this view of a need for increased order is particularly pronounced in those areas that adopt private security, or whether it is a widespread refrain. Hough and Mayhew (op. cit., p. 28) found that only half the respondents in the British Crime Survey thought that offenders should be brought to court and most favoured only fines as a penalty. Only 10 per cent of all respondents thought that a custodial sentence was appropriate for offenders and only 2 per cent favoured corporal punishment. The British Crime Survey showed that much crime goes unreported. These writers concluded that this large incidence of unreported crime was not evidence of a contemporary breakdown of order, on the contrary, it had existed for as long as criminal statistics have been collected. Hough and Mayhew (op. cit., pp. 32-33) in analysing their research, thus, dismiss the idea that people's tolerance of crime has decreased. These findings would tend to indicate that public attitudes did not show any noticeable increase concerning demands for more public order. However, as Hough (1989, p. 51) points out, the social stratification of police users as respondents has an important bearing upon the outcome of the data collected. This is relevant to the present study as the sample contained mostly middle-class respondents who may be expected to seek an increase in public order. In contrast, a number of polls offer support for the belief that people generally favour a tougher approach by the courts (Gallup, 1982; Marplan, 1983). It cannot be established with any certainty, however, that a need for order is more pronounced in areas where private security patrol is used, but it may be accepted that this attitude has some influence upon the instigation of private security patrol.

Motivation: a dual process

The empirical findings in this part of the research point-up three dominant and interrelated factors concerning the motivation for private security patrol. The first relates to a particular concern by residents for increased levels of crime, and or, minor incidents of disorder. Secondly, due to crime increases, residents perceived a need for additional police protection but the method which they believed would be most effective - enhanced patrol - was not publicly available to them. Linked to these factors was the general feeling that community order was breaking down and needed reinforcing. There is, thus, a strong social element within the motive for private patrols. The impact which private individuals had upon change cannot, therefore, be underestimated. Thirdly, in addition to the influence of human agency, there is a structural element present, for there is evidence of motivation being affected by state policy on crime control - self help and freedom of choice. It is appropriate to discuss these matters further and make distinctions about particular influences in each case study.

If police resources on the streets of the research sites had decreased then there appears to be a positive relationship between crime-rates and police resources (Carr-Hill and Stern, 1979). In effect, an increase in crime occurred but there was an absence of effective policing to control it - the dominant state policy being self-help and freedom of choice. Protection by private security patrol thus became the rational alternative. There is, ironically, just a chance that rising crime rates may have some connection with increased numbers of police - although there appears to be ample evidence that police discover only a small amount of recorded crime (Bottomley and Coleman, op. cit.; Mawby, op. cit.; Black, 1970, 1971). In contemporary times there does also appear to be a feeling amongst the public of intolerance to police ineffectiveness. An apparent lack of effort and impoliteness are some of the complaints made about police officer's performance today. Percentages of respondents who complained of such matters concerning police effectiveness have been high (Skogan, 1990, pp. 16-18). Another consideration concerning the rise in crime reported to police must also be that the public today are obliged to make such reports for insurance purposes.

At Moston and Bridton there was evidence of a high level of economic power amongst individual residents. This also existed at Becton to a lesser extent - especially in the poorer area of the high-rise flats where the patrol spent most time. The more economically powerful were able to create their own destiny by defining their community policing needs through the use of private security. This was less apparent at Becton where New Right policies on crime control emanated more from the council than from individuals - evidence 19 per cent of the household sample being unaware that the patrol existed. Private security, at Moston and Bridton in particular, strongly possessed a mandate defined by clients (Shearing and Stenning, 1983, pp. 498-502). Because private individuals are the main users of security-services a client defined mandate is unsurprising (Shearing, Farnell and Stenning, 1980, p. 163). In relation to the creation of policing, it is interesting to note that because 'communities' authorize the use of force in regulating internal affairs it is possible to create formal institutions of government and law without developing public police. Thus an essential element of police is 'authorization in the name of the community' (Bayley, 1986, p. 23).

It is, accordingly, the 'sustainers' who are influential in defining the police's 'key practice' (Cain, 1979, p. 4; Bittner, 1970, Chap. 6). Flexibility and width of investigation into the concept of 'police' is thus allowed as 'the' public police ceases to be the dominant factor. Included in this more sociologically energetic definition is the right for a variety of forces, including private security, to share functional aspects of policing (Chaiken and Chaiken, op. cit.). This right emanates not only from the power of the state but from the public's courteous regard to it (Berger, Berger and Kellner, op. cit.; Giddens, 1981, 1984).

Another significant factor in this part of the research is the contrast between the data found at Moston/Bridton and Becton which tends to indicate that a lesser need existed at Becton for private patrol services. This is evident in the fact that Becton residents appeared relatively satisfied with the level of public policing they received. This was clearly not the case at Moston and Bridton. It could be argued, therefore, that the installation of the private patrol at Becton was not at the instigation of the residents but the council. These distinguishing factors, outlined between the research sites, tend to support the subjective evidence of coercive elements in Becton Council.

State policy on crime-control would, therefore, appear to be an important influence on both individual and organizational motivation to provide personal protection. This alternative fitted well to the policy adopted by Becton Council, for there is some evidence that they used the demand for protection to perpetuate their ideology for free market forces and public choice. This conclusion, however, needs further consideration. It must be seen against the fact that the state has been spending more and more on crime control and that numbers of police have increased significantly. If the state favours market solutions to police provision the question has to be asked why is it spending so much on public police? It must also be said that most councils have not followed Becton's policy of private provision of policing.

It has been shown in this chapter that the motivation for change was not due simply to one influence - either the state or the subjects within it. It is apparent that both these factors are present. This obviously requires an understanding of change which allows for the duality of agency and structure; a duality best described in the concept of 'structuration' (Giddens, 1979). As a concept structuration expresses the mutual dependency of human agency and social structure. Social structures are intimately involved in the production of action by individuals.

5 Community and functional characteristics

In this chapter the nature and characteristics of the communities in which private security patrols operate are identified. Analysis is made in context with the idea of 'community crime prevention' and conclusions are drawn concerning patrols' relation to 'community' as an integral part of the preventative ideal on a macro level. The primary functions and method of the patrols are also examined. To obtain this objective I collected data from interviews, documents and participant observation. Asset protection was found to be a primary objective of the patrol and surveillance the primary method of their operation.

The symbolic community

Although situational crime prevention strategies will be more successful in communities where people are worried about crime and where they feel positive towards their neighbour (Hope, 1988, p. 159) there is a lack of success in neighbourhood schemes both nationally (Hough and Mayhew, 1983) and internationally (Whitaker, 1986). Furthermore:

> Crime prevention is also ethically wrong because it is the very antithesis of what living in a law abiding society should be all about. It is a law for the rich who can afford security and no law at all for the old and poor people who so often feature in the crime reports. When men first began to live together in communities one of the prime reasons was for mutual security. Crime prevention abandons that concept and says it is every man for himself - the law of the jungle. (Worsley, 1983, p. 22).

And at each research site in the present study I similarly found ample evidence to indicate a general failure of care in the community and the dominance of individualism amongst residents.

It was shown earlier that the neighbourhood watch scheme at Moston was ineffective - nothing more than a symbolic gesture at 'community' (Hunter, op. cit.). At Bridton no neighbourhood watch scheme existed. This absence of communal spirit may be seen as reflecting residents' lack of interest in a self-caring community. When the subject of local neighbourhood watch schemes was brought up during interviews, residents constantly told me that communal disinterest was the reason for lack of success. There was no suggestion that respondents' antipathy to neighbourhood watch type schemes was due to the fact that they already had a private security scheme.

The same apathy existed at Becton. Tenants' interests were represented by a few residents who were members of the Tenants' Association. At a regularly held police and community consultative committee meeting, which I attended at Becton, I noticed that only one representative from the Rams Council Estate was present. This man was a neighbourhood watch co-ordinator for a small area on the estate. I considered him to be middle-class (Lavrakas et al, 1980; Skogan and Maxfield, op. cit.; Wandersman, Jakubs and Giamartino, op. cit.) and unrepresentative of the many families who resided in the Rams Estate Flats. Like the few crime prevention enthusiasts - 'prime movers' - at Moston and Bridton, this man had a charismatic and participating personality and was seriously concerned about the state of local crime (Kasarda and Janowitz, op. cit.; Hunter, op. cit.).

At all sites the social characteristics of those who became involved in crime prevention correlated with the more participating individual (Hope, op. cit. p. 158). Thus most residents, although concerned about crime, did not become actively engaged in prevention (Turk, op. cit. p. 141; Hope, ibid., p.148). If a caring community correlates with successful collective, preventative schemes then the answer for the uncaring communities that I had found was to contract-in a protection agency.

At all sites I found that those who did participate seriously towards the inception of the private patrol exhibited higher levels of informal social interaction in the neighbourhood than those who did not participate (Kasarda and Janowitz, op. cit.; Hunter, op. cit.). Furthermore, this tendency to participate was occurring in a predominately middle-class environment (Lavrakas et al, 1980; Skogan and Maxfield, ibid.; Wandersman, Jakubs and Giamartino, op. cit.). Thus, it was evident that this crime prevention strategy was more likely to develop in neighbourhoods with economic and moral homogeneity (Greenberg, Rohe and Williams, op. cit.). Middle-class neighbourhoods feel more control over their environments and are more responsive to self-help strategies and less reliant on police than typical lower-class neighbourhoods (Boggs, 1971; Greenberg, Rohe and Williams, op. cit.; Hackler, Ho and Urquhart-Ross, op. cit.; Taub, Taylor and Dunham, op. cit.; Taylor, Gottfredson and Brower, 1981). Regardless of any attitudinal class difference the fundamental fact remains that middle-class people can better afford private provision.

Absence and bad neighbours

At Moston and Bridton I found that most residents were absent from home during the daytime due to their employment. Mothers with young children were the usual family members seen about during daytime. For the purposes of my interview schedule it was more productive to visit homes in the evening when most family members were available for interview. This 'absence' may not be uncommon in such areas of privately owned property where unemployment is low and most households have dual wage earners.

Thus the type of neighbourhood in which I found myself researching became clearly identifiable through my participation with residents as I met and spoke to them in the streets or in their homes. The neighbourhood was predominantly characterized by the centrality of commodity production, distribution and exchange - residents' market relationships were pre-eminent. Residents clearly associated social status with the area in which they lived and their property. The protection of their property - and hence their status - through the installation of private security patrol seemed to be interrelated in some way. The patrol was a part of residents' guarantee of securing this status in the broader community and it set them apart from other communities who did not have this additional protection. Indeed, in a few cases I found that some residents had been influenced to move into the area because of the patrol's existence and talked about the patrol in the context of 'snob value'.

It has been argued that the primacy of market relations in this type of community tends to create class societies where the social status of the area is as important as the social status of the individual (Rutter and Giller, 1983, p. 206). Other writers have claimed that the change in style of neighbourhood policing from public to private is partly due to this phenomenon and is a characteristic of middle-class neighbourhoods (Sherman, op. cit., p. 148). Such a community and policing style is unlikely to increase neighbour contact and promote communal feeling. There is an overwhelming analysis in social research that as community care declines other services will advance (Keller, 1968). Even if surveillance was likely on its own to curtail crime, community watch schemes cannot be easily implemented and maintained in all neighbourhoods (Rosenbaum, 1988, p. 142).

Accordingly, the type of neighbourhood examined in this study is unlikely, by the very absence of their inhabitants during working hours, to provide successful self-administered watch schemes. My own impressions of the existence of an apparent lack of social interaction, supported by some evidence of residents' non-communicability, strengthens that claim. Indeed, successful community care is uncommon and improbable in contemporary society - for in advanced capitalism the combination of market moralities and official services act against it. Some argue that there exists the 'economics of bad neighbours' (Keller, ibid.; Hirsch, 1977, pp. 71-83) and the 'society of strangers' (Merry, 1981; Ignatieff, 1983). Here a negative relationship is created which has an economic logic. This can best be seen in the fact that it would logically appear that public policing is costly but, alternatively, neighbourliness is very cheap. However, from the point of view of the individual capitalist this position is reversed - neighbourliness is costly (as it impinges upon his lifestyle and ability to maintain status levels) and public police costs, unavoidably paid through the tax precept, are low (Abrams, 1977, p. 80). This theoretical position supports the view that ideal preventative strategies should have more to do with large rather than small solutions to combat the reality of inequitable current public policy (Yin, 1986, p. 308). It would ask also for a greater recognition that, to some extent, society's crime problems can be described within the 'crisis of capitalism' framework (Platt and Takagi, 1981, pp. 30-58).

If the economics of bad neighbours argument is at all correct then such neighbourhoods as studied here depend strongly upon continuing publicly provided services. It seems sensible, therefore, that if these publicly provided services are seen as defective then private protection will have to be the only alternative - better to pay for effective protection than attempt to provide it on a community basis by impracticable and ineffective neighbourhood watch schemes.

Keeping 'them' out: community fragmentation

Neighbourhood private security schemes are either private, in the sense that clients are private owners of property, or public, in that councils have developed schemes to protect publicly owned housing. This distinction between public and private property is, however, less relevant than appears at first sight. For instance, the council at Becton provide a security patrol for homes which, although once publicly owned, are now 75 per cent owner-occupied. This can hardly be seen as representative of a poorer area. However, it must be noted that at Becton I collected more critical comments from respondents about the private patrol than I did at the other two sites. Although, in the main, Becton residents were economically advantaged, they were not as highly advantaged as residents at the other two sites. The areas of low owner occupation at Becton consisted mainly of blocks of flats - the residents of which were identified by many respondents as a threat to their property. These flats were less physically attractive to purchase and had more crime problems than elsewhere on the Rams Estate. The economically disadvantaged tended to be lumped together in these areas where crime was high (Roshier, op. cit., p. 94). Nevertheless, there was a general affluence amongst Becton residents. The distinction I draw between class identification at and the other two sites may best be described as being upper working class and upper middle class respectively.

Although councils such as Becton are concerned for the quality of life of their tenants, of more serious concern was found to be the opportunity reduction of crimes against council property and the financial saving this would provide (Skogan, 1988, p. 39). This concern for financial loss through crime was evident in my enquiries and the explanations given by councils which operated private patrol. The paramount concern of councils for loss reduction is significant in that it too correlates with government ideology on effectiveness and efficiency. In striving for economy councils increasingly utilise the protective services of the private security industry. The individual owner-occupier respondents too, like council executives, were primarily concerned for the opportunity reduction of crime against their property. Thus not only the characteristic of impersonality existed at research sites, the class nature of the social order was also evident. Modern capitalism may not only have the capacity to create a society of strangers but may also give rise to the birth of class (Perkin, 1969; Giddens, 1973, pp. 132-135; 1981, pp. 76-217).

In order to test the wider implications of integrative community attitudes from a subjective position, respondents at all research sites were asked to identify their perceptions of the domicile of those who offended in their area. In each case there was a predominance towards naming areas within the local council estates. At Moston, those interviewed identified a particular Council Estate, 'Blackbank', as the location from which offenders came. At Bridton a specific Council Estate called 'Kelton', was named as the problem area. For Becton residents offenders came from 'the flats'. On average, 75 per cent of respondents identified local areas of inferior housing as being the homes of those responsible for their crime problems.

Protective behaviour through small efforts does not enhance the security of a wider community. Such behaviour acts to fragment rather than integrate society. Respondents' perceptions of the location of the threat to safety from those residing on local public housing estates, and other less fortunate residential areas than their own, reinforces the polarisation of communities. Some communities have defined boundaries because all the adjacent communities disclaim their residents. These residential enclaves acquire an identity and a set of boundaries simply because they are left out of others (Suttles, op. cit., pp. 240-241). Thus, a 'symbolic' community assumes a 'we versus they' attitude. The primary objective of this style of community is the protection of 'your' area to prevent 'them' getting in. 'They' are not part of 'your' community (Currie, 1988, p. 281).

Fear and community polarization

When crime is associated with the less well-off, and this is reinforced by segregated housing patterns and an emphasis on different value structures, the result can be an escalation of the fear of crime and an increase in segregation (Conklin, op. cit., pp. 33-34). Furthermore, the ever-increasing trend to seek out protection from outside agencies may only increase feelings of insecurity and create fragmented, self-perpetuating communities:

> Paradoxically, the more we enter into relationships to obtain the security commodity, the more insecure we feel; the more we depend upon the commodity rather than each other to keep us safe and confident, the less safe and confident we feel; the more we divide the world into those who are able to enhance our security and those who threaten it, the less we are able to provide it for ourselves......The 'quest for security' through the market thus not only sets us apart from each other and leads us to see those beyond the commodity relationship as threats rather than resources, it may also directly contribute to a sense of insecurity as well. (Spitzer, 1987, p. 50).

Thus, 'respectable fears' affect policies towards those areas and communities which are deprived (Hall et al, 1978; Pearson, 1983). Reacting to panic over increasing disorder is seen as a distraction away from the more serious problems in society. The fear of crime can serve as a way of legitimizing and rationalising increased control of subordinate populations (Merry, op. cit., p.

220). Concern about crime thus justifies and reinforces hostility that stems from class conflict.

As society becomes more complex it is harder to identify and isolate those who want to damage it. And, if my analysis is accurate, private provision, through non-participative schemes such as private security patrol, will tend to confuse this issue further by creating greater differences amongst already fragmented classes. Thus pockets of private security protection would seem only to strengthen the dysfunctional aspects of 'community' as an ideal:

> The pursuit of justice by individuals as well as by groups leads to creation of larger systems of discipline that destroy the vitality of small-scale communities. By militating against community the quest for justice often generates the need for more extensive interference at a later stage, but then not in the interests of justice but of order. (Bayley, 1980, p. 54).

It remains a natural instinct to protect whatever property we possess no matter what neighbourhood we live in. This instinct requires positive action and people will defend themselves given the right physical framework (Newman, op. cit.). However, if shown to be effective, the crime prevention through residential design model not only controls the regulation of predatory behaviour it also places emphasis on the sanctity of private property. It concerns a further responsibility of those with an interest in maintaining private property to police those who have no such stake.

The strategy of private security patrol, thus, reinforces the power of those who own property and it reinforces the fear they feel towards the propertyless (Boostrom and Henderson, op. cit., p. 28; Suttles, op. cit.). Financially weak sections of the community tend to be identified on a 'cognitive map', as areas from where 'predatory', 'shiftless' and 'desperate' characters emanate (Suttles, ibid., p. 33). Social divisions between the 'haves' and the 'have nots' creates a class separate from that class labelled as deviant.

Similar communities to those found in this study have rallied around stereotyped fears of the poor, assuming their criminality and reacting to it by increased defensive actions (Stuart, 1970, p. 2). An important determinant of defended boundaries is, therefore, the notion of financial loss reduction by keeping out those seen as a threat to the financial interests of the better-off in the community. This gives assurance of peaceableness and a durable community to those who want and can afford it (Suttles, ibid., p. 241). Thus here there is support for the notion that political power in society tends to be possessed by a small homogeneous elite who psychologically adapt well to social and economic change (Pareto, op. cit.; Mosca, 1939). Seen in this light, the communities where private security patrol operate are the very antithesis of communities of organic solidarity (Durkheim, 1897). Such elitist communities, where the classical ethic of self-help and public choice has a strong influence, are likely as a creation to have been influenced both by the state (Cohen, op. cit., p. 123) and the individual community member (Berger, and Luckman, 1967; Berger, Berger and Kellner, op. cit.; Giddens, 1979, 1984).

Functional characteristics are now considered.

Property protection

The monotonous regularity with which I found patrol personnel carried out property checks indicated the functional dominance of the security of property (Shearing and Stenning, 1983; South, 1987a, 1987b). My observations, thus, identified the main concern of the Moston and Bridton patrol to be the safety of residents' private property and, in the case of the Becton patrol, the safety of council-owned property.

An array of valuables was constantly visible in the areas patrolled. In addition to high value housing on the Moston and Bridton sites there were a considerable number of two, three, and in some cases, four-car-families. At Bridton Brian regularly commented on the total value of all the un-garaged motor cars parked on the streets and reminded me that vehicles were the highest valued possessions left outside to tempt the thief.

The tower blocks of the Rams Estate at Becton bear witness to the contemporary reconstruction of the urban environment. The had structural characteristics which tend to lend themselves to the use of private security patrols. I found that environmental security was being affected by socio-economic trends, which in turn had changed patterns of access to property (South, 1987b, p. 149) by displacing public and allowing in private policing agencies (Shearing and Stenning, 1981, p. 229).

Possessions remained a constant topic of conversation throughout the time I accompanied patrols. These observations were confirmed by the subjective data collected from interviews. A negative response from the Becton sample underlined a general ineffectiveness concerning that patrol scheme. There may have been a number of reasons for such a negative response from Becton respondents. It is necessary to outline these in order that the often considerable differences between the responses from Becton residents and those at the other two sites can be analysed satisfactorily.

Firstly, Becton patrol's maintenance reports related to the tower-block flats more than any other area of the estate. This may indicate that the non-owner-occupier area, which still remained the primary responsibility of the council, was the main target of the patrol. If the main job of the patrol was keeping an eye on this rougher council property it may not be surprising that residents who did not reside there, and presumably did not receive as much attention, saw the patrol as ineffective. At times when I worked with the patrol at Becton I was aware that the area of the flats was given more attention. But this was mainly because the flats area was where most problems existed. The responsibility of the patrol, nevertheless, was to the entire estate and they did not just patrol the flats. Secondly, the considerable support for the local public police found at Becton may have been associated with respondents' opposition to the privatisation of policing and, thus, their objection to the patrol. Thirdly, it is worth remembering that in contrast to the relatively smaller geographical areas of Moston and Bridton, where smaller local firms provided the patrol, the Becton patrol had a much larger area of responsibility and a comparatively small number of personnel employed by a nationally run company. In contrast, data from Moston and Bridton showed the patrols' protective ability was valued (Reiss, 1983, 1987). This contrast is often duplicated throughout the study.

Concern and fear: the psychological utility of patrol

In addition to identifying the physical aspect of the patrol's function, I sought to identify any emotional effects the patrol was having on residents. In estimating the level of fear or concern felt by residents the effects upon them of the historical events they had experienced were considered. The high levels of concern felt by residents, created by the incidents of trespass into their homes and to other property, has application in defining their overall feelings. When this factor is taken into consideration it can be seen that residents' emotions consisted of elements of both fear and serious concern for themselves and their property. This level of emotion is consistent with a definition of fear which can be created by the loss of property (Garofalo, op. cit.).

In order to test the hypothesis that private security patrol allays the fear of crime (Donovan and Walsh, op. cit. p. 61) I designed part of the questionnaire to include residents' views of the patrols' most important function, as distinct from identifying the primary area of enhanced protection. Property protection could have been expected to dominate this response, however, the provision of a 'feeling of security' rated high at both

Moston and Bridton. At Becton the response was very negative. This may be accountable by the larger geographical area which the Becton patrol covered. Additionally, the Becton area was more urbanised than the other two sites. It would logically follow from this that providing a feeling of security in such an urbanised area would be much more difficult than in the less urbanised areas of Moston and Bridton. The value of 'deterrence' to residents at all sites was also very evident in the present study (Donovan and Walsh, ibid. p. 44). The extent of demand for a deterrent, proactive policing style is important for traditional policing (Reiss, 1983, 1987). Thus, in the present study a correlation was found between emphasis on foot patrol and decreasing fears of crime (Skogan, 1987). This finding, which suggests the need for an increase in the symbolic role of public policing, is matched by the findings of other research:

> The fourth and, probably most important role which the public demanded was the symbolic one of, by their very presence, proclaiming a state of order. This was the root of the wish, noted in many other studies, for more foot patrols. 'Panda Cars', or their latter-day equivalents, provided the public with little reassurance. (Shapland and Vagg, 1988, p. 149).

In addition to the safety residents may have felt in a general sense, the study sought to test how safe residents felt when out alone at night in the streets of the patrolled area, as opposed to an unpatrolled area. Notwithstanding the fact that the primary target for protection is property, the finding from this question illustrated the feeling of enhanced personal safety felt by residents when in the streets at Moston and Bridton. It confirms residents' legitimation of the patrols' public disorder-deterrent function, if only in a symbolic sense (Donovan and Walsh, op. cit. pp. 56-60). The reassuring presence engendered by the patrols at Moston and Bridton is absent in the response I obtained to the Becton patrol. As noted in the previous data, this could be accounted for by the more urbanised area of Becton when compared to the other two sites. As none of the research sites suffered from special public disorder problems this response of 'reassurance' can be viewed merely as part of the symbolic effects of patrol.

The overall response provided evidence of the indispensability of the private service to residents at Moston and Bridton. In contrast, at Becton, the patrol was not seen as having much impact upon the safety of the community. Indeed, 38 per cent of households were unaware of the patrol's existence. However, nearly 40 per cent of the Becton sample who were aware of the patrol felt they would be worse off if they did not have it.

Police invisibility

Residents' feelings of insecurity can be correlated with the absence of regular patrolling of officers, especially on foot. Residents were concerned at the 'invisibility' of police and many stated that regular and visible public police patrols would have considerably enhanced their feelings of security (Shapland and Vagg, op. cit.). Although a question had not been specifically designed to test this response the subject was regularly brought up by respondents during interviews. In view of this a note was made on each occasion that a respondent referred to this concern. The data collected in this way showed considerable concern by residents for the lack of police patrol in the areas - 53.6 per cent at Moston, 39.8 per cent at Bridton and 22.3 per cent at Becton were concerned.

It is appropriate here to again recall the geographical differences between the research sites - for this factor must affect residents' perceptions of visible public police patrol. It may be quite possible that persons residing in a cul de sac, like Moston, would not see as many patrolling officers as those who resided on a main thoroughfare. Furthermore, it could be expected that in highly urbanised areas, such as Becton, the level of concern for crime and disorder may be higher than in more rural areas such as Moston and Bridton. It would follow, therefore, that the tendency for reassurance through visible patrol may be higher in the more urban areas. However, concerning this last point, the data collected here shows that respondents in the less urbanised areas were more concerned about the lack of public police visibility.

A major finding from these responses further points to the importance of the psychological advantage that residents obtain from knowing that someone is watching out. The fundamental message which I was receiving from respondents was that people needed to feel safe and secure. Foot patrol gives this assurance of security. High profile foot patrols, apart from any practical value which they perform, added to the quality of life of the residents. The actual presence of someone watching-out, and challenging strangers diplomatically, may have a stronger psychological effect than alarms, locks and other such preventative devices. The importance of the empirical finding that a sense of security was not being provided by the public police needs further emphasis. This shows that the need for reassurance is behind both the public call for more police and the public acceptance of political cries for more money for police:

When the man in the street asks for more police he is really asking for the police to be on hand more frequently and more conspicuously when he is going about his daily business. (Bahan, 1974, pp. 340-341).

There is growing support for the view that public police can play an important role in controlling the fear of crime. Research does show that the presence of police on the streets is associated with feelings of safety (Balkin and Houlden, 1983). Furthermore, residents with high confidence in the public police are generally less fearful than those with low confidence (Baker et al, 1983) and their confidence is increased by 'directed patrol' (Cordner, 1986; Pate and Wycoff, 1986; Trojanowicz, 1986). Directed patrolling means that, in order to improve patrol effectiveness, officers work with clearly defined objectives at times when they are not responding to calls for assistance and other tasks. Emphasis is placed on officers' supervisors targeting relevant patrol areas and directing officers accordingly (Burrows and Lewis, 1988). Thus, if supervisors are aware of elderly residents' fear due to some recent criminal event, they instruct patrolling officers to give more attention to that area. It is important that such residents see the police as able to provide protection through patrol, for research has shown a relationship exists between the perceived adequacy of police protection and the subjective likelihood of personal victimization (Baumer, op. cit.).

However, the reduction of fear is no substitute for the reduction of crime - but it may be very important to that type of culture where the sense of social structure and public responsibility for coping with social problems is underdeveloped (Currie, op. cit., p. 282). Communities with weakened informal control systems - such as those in the present study - exacerbate conditions in which crime may flourish, (Moore and Brown, 1981, p. 26; Maxfield, op. cit.) thereafter, levels of crime and disorder serve as signs of crime and may lead to fear regardless of actual levels of crime (Wilson and Kelling, 1982). It should be noted, however, that it may be unrealistic to expect the total elimination of fear. Furthermore, its elimination is undesirable because of fear's functional ability to lead individuals to take precautions (Garofalo, op. cit., p. 856).

The research findings of others, outlined here, on the physical presence of police and allaying of fear may appear conclusive. However, there was evidence in the present study that the relationships involved in the process of allaying crime were more complex than they appeared. Criminal victimization is only one variable in the experience of fear. There were other, less direct experiences which were likely to affect the daily lives of residents. These indirect influences are now identified.

Protection entrepreneurs: communication and the perpetuation of fear

> They speak to me a lot. They tell me about the local crime and how we should watch out for this and that. I don't believe they have any effect. They're just making sure they keep the job here. If it wasn't for my wife I wouldn't have them. (Moston Resident).

During observations at Moston and Bridton I identified several instances where patrol personnel's conversations with clients may have heightened the fear of crime. It became apparent to me that residents' perceptions of the threat to their personal safety, and that of their property, was being influenced by these conversations. The effective liaison between the patrol and the police was an important factor here. I found that the police, having minute to minute information on reported crime and disorder, were apprising the private patrolmen on some of these incidents. Some of this information was subsequently used by the patrol to 'educate' their clients on specific themes of prevention. Of the many occasions in which I was present during conversations between patrolmen and their clients there were few when such educative warnings were not given.

While I was accompanying a patrolman at Moston we stopped to talk to a lady who was in her garden. The conversation turned to local crime and the patrolman pointed out that there was a local gang of thieves who were travelling around on motor cycles and breaking into premises. The message was that she should look out for this gang. I wondered how this lady, or others in the community, may benefit from this information. There was just a chance that she may see a gang of youths using motor cycles and report it to the police - hopefully the police would then arrest the youths and prosecute them. Alternatively, and more realistically perhaps, she may never positively identify the suspicious group of motor cyclists and continually be concerned of their possible presence nearby.

One evening while patrolling with Brian on the Bridton Estate a female resident approached us. She told us that during the previous evening, an attempt had been made to steal from her motor car which had been parked on the drive of her home. Having noted the information Brian proceeded to describe incidents involving a spate of local thefts and burglaries in surrounding estates. If I had been a resident on the estate this warning would have increased my fear of crime occurring. While I was able to understand the need to warn this resident about potential threats to her property I found it ironic that there was a possibility fear could be generated by the protecting agent himself.

87

In relation to these educative warnings given by patrolmen, a particular conversation between myself and Brian is of interest. Having completed an analysis of the crime pattern on the Bridton Estate I discussed the results with Brian. The analysis showed that crime in the patrolled area was low in contrast to the area not patrolled - a success which could reasonably be attributed to Brian. However, this posed an apparent problem for Brian which made me feel uneasy. He told me that if his clients believed the crime rate had decreased they may feel they did not need his protection any longer. I became equally concerned that my research findings would jeopardize the access Brian had allowed me. Thus, I found myself attempting to persuade Brian that he need not worry because I would not be divulging my findings to his clients.

While interviewing residents at Moston and Bridton I attempted to further clarify the effects that conversations were having on residents' perceptions of local levels of crime. On each occasion that a response indicated perceptions of crime in the local area was high, I prompted the respondent by asking: 'How do you know that?' Over 50 per cent of those questioned thought that their perceptions of high levels of local crime were the result of what they were told by patrolmen - a considerable influence upon residents' fear of crime.

A further example of the effects of residents' concern about the crime problem at Moston related to the tendency to non-communication between neighbours mentioned earlier. There were two adjoining households not participating in the scheme. One family had refused to join the scheme from the beginning, the other had initially joined but later withdrew. The geographical position of these premises is relevant - they were end properties, situated at the entrance to the estate and at the opposite end of the street to where most of the problems had occurred. In a neighbourhood which was not high in community interactions both these families were seen by other neighbours as particularly unsociable. Indeed, when interviewed, they concurred on the opinion of their un-neighbourliness. One family had initially joined the scheme reluctantly after being approached by others living at the other end of the street. Only then did they discover there were problems of crime and disorder in the street. Thus their lack of sociability had created the effect which occurs when an ostrich puts its head in the sand. After a few months, however, they left the scheme believing it was unnecessary for their purposes. The findings of Garofalo (op. cit.) and Skogan and Maxfield (op. cit.) are relevant to this part of the study. The effects of communicability between patrol-persons and residents, or indeed its non-existence between neighbours, were apparent in perceptions and attitudes to fear - for the less distant or abstract the message, the greater its consequences for fear (Skogan and Maxfield, op. cit., p. 11). Thus 'fear-exacerbation', (Greenberg, Rohe and Williams, op. cit.; Rosenbaum, op. cit., p. 136) where fear increases due to exchanges of information on local crime, clearly existed at Moston and Bridton and were created through conversations between patrol-persons and residents.

Position in social space, particularly applicable to neighbours at Moston, is another important factor concerning the amount and nature of information about crime to which the person is exposed. The image of crime held by an individual has a number of elements, extent, nature and consequences. These images tell the individual about the source of the threat and from where it is coming (Garofalo, op. cit., p. 844). Skogan and Maxfield (op. cit. p. 113) show how urban dwellers in Chicago, Philadelphia and San Francisco coped with the problems of fear and crime. They concluded that fear is indeed a consequence of crime but that most consequences of crime, including fear, are indirect. So, apart from direct victimization, there are other contacts that will influence public fear - such as conversation with other victims, the mass media and neighbourhood conditions. Garofalo's (ibid.) findings, and those of the present study, also concur with the work of Conklin (1971, p. 374) who describes individuals in these situations as 'indirect victims' whose attitudes and behaviour change through knowledge without 'direct victimisation'.

Fear of crime is clearly a complex psychological matter on which there is much debate. It is obviously unsatisfactory to investigate the problem from a purely criminal justice/criminology basis. There is a need, additionally, to let into the examination some basic psychological and social-psychological reasoning. Paradoxically the 'client updating' process described earlier tended to have a dual and contradictory effect upon residents. For not only did it legitimize the patrol's 'fear reducing' function, it perpetuated fear and thus insecurity. Here, therefore, was evidence both of subjective, emotional influences concerning the patrol's function (Berger, Berger and Kellner, op. cit.; Giddens, 1981, 1984, 1991) and professionals' exploitation of the opportunity of the state to use new techniques and knowledge to construct preventative strategies against deviance (Cohen, op. cit.).

Specific functions of private patrol

The extent to which particular traditional public police functions were being carried out by the private patrol is addressed in this section. To attain this objective I obtained the views of residents, observed the patrol during their normal duties and examined documents relating to clients' functional requirements of the patrol. I aimed to identify specific functions as well as examining the extent to which force was used by the patrol - especially force concerning public disorder.

The primary matters which residents reported to both the local police and the private patrol concerned, security of premises left unoccupied (30 per cent), suspicious incidents (20 per cent), minor theft (10 per cent) and nuisance (10 per cent). Although the majority of respondents at all sites said they did not only report matters to the private patrol, the data showed there was an overlap of some of the private agency's functions into certain areas of traditional public provision. Before discussing these four areas in more detail it will be helpful to contextualise the data to some degree by showing the types of incident which residents routinely reported to the police but not to the private security guards. No fundamental variation in the classification of these incidents existed at the three sites; other than at Moston, where I did not find reports of assaults or woundings. The more usual types of incident reported only to police were, therefore, burglary, assaults/woundings, theft of (or from) vehicles, thefts of all other items, criminal damage and nuisance.

Unoccupied premises

In the interest of individual property-rights the public police have always felt particular responsibility for the security of unoccupied premises. Protecting unoccupied premises was by far the most common function which residents reported only to the private patrol. In addition to the interview data my observations at Moston and Bridton confirmed that patrol personnel did pay particular attention to unoccupied premises - especially when occupants were away on holiday. This is further illustrated at Moston by reference to the patrol's incident logs where I found regular recording of this function. From observations at Becton I found there were some council owned premises which were unoccupied for short periods of time. Patrolmen were aware of these and checked their security. I found no evidence, however, that special attention was given to them. At Becton no respondent informed private patrolmen when leaving premises unoccupied or going away on holiday. This is supported by the absence of such reports in the patrol incident logs.

Suspicious incidents

From interview data and records I found that at Moston there were instances in which residents reported suspicious incidents to patrol personnel without informing the police. These often related to strange persons or vehicles in the street. The incidents were often seen by respondents as not important enough to report to the police. To report such incidents to the private patrolmen assured residents that future recurrences would at least be given attention by the patrol, who were always nearby. During observations at Moston I witnessed occasions when residents reported particular incidents to the patrol. These consisted, again, of strange vehicles seen in the street. I noted later that this information had not been recorded in the incident logs. When I questioned these omissions a patrolman told me that a good deal of information was kept in his head to be subsequently passed on verbally to his colleagues. Thus numerical data obtained from security logs may only have been conservative estimates. It is important to note that the information received by the security guards was largely lost to the police and any kind of official knowledge.

At Bridton I found that Brian's sociable personality often encouraged residents to report matters they had seen. During observations there were several occasions when I witnessed such conversations. The matters usually referred to cars and persons seen in the area and not identified as 'local' by residents. I found no evidence at Becton that residents were reporting such matters to the private patrol.

Minor theft

Residents at all sites were not regularly reporting incidents of theft only to the private patrol. However, one respondent at Moston and three at Bridton had reported some thefts only to them. These four incidents related to the theft of low value items such as children's toys left unattended in gardens and conifers uprooted and removed from garden borders.

Nuisance

Nuisance is a broad term. In the police service it is probably most associated with public complaints of a minor, non-violent nature - anything from noise in the street to indecent exposure. A large proportion of nuisance offences and incidents concern the 'soft' or 'service' function of policing. Before the inception of the Moston patrol there were instances of nuisance which caused concern for residents. Residents felt the presence of the patrol had resolved these problems and my observations confirmed this. Furthermore, I found no evidence of these nuisances recurring at Moston. There were no reports of nuisance made to the Bridton patrol. Police records showed there were very few problems of nuisance reported at all. The estate just did not have a nuisance problem. At Becton there were many reports of nuisance

91

made to me during my research on the Rams Estate. Some of Becton Council's Estate Managers had told me how they believed the community was often reluctant to complain to the police about matters which included the 'service' function of policing. These complaints, they said, were increasingly being made to the council and not to the police. Such complaints regularly concerned incidents involving public nuisance or damage to property. An example which was given to me concerned an elderly lady living alone on the Rams Estate. She had telephoned the council to report that youths were harassing her - she had been singled out as a gypsy by them. Some of the problems she experienced from the youths included verbal abuse outside her house and dog excrement being placed through her letter-box. The council employee taking the complaint asked the lady if she had reported these matters to the police and was told she had not. The elderly lady explained that if she did report the matters to the police those responsible would make things worse for her. She was, therefore, appealing to the council for help as one of their tenants in the hope they could resolve the problem.

To suggest that the reason which inhibited the old lady from reporting harassment to the police also applied to others who failed to report raises a general methodological issue. This concerns the need to produce area-based variations on the inclination to report to the police. Contextual data on levels of reporting to police at research sites was collected during conversations I had with respondents and other residents. At all locations my clear impressions were that residents normally reported most criminal activity to the police. Some criminal disorder incidents which were not reported to police consisted of minor theft and nuisances. At Becton, however, I was more aware that residents were less likely to report incidents of nuisance to the police. This may not be surprising considering the geographical size of Becton in comparison to the other two sites and the volume of police- work that this larger area was likely to create. Indeed, during conversations with police officers at Becton I discovered that Becton police had discontinued recording these types of routine beat complaints. This was not the case for Moston and Bridton police. This tendency demonstrated that Becton police had not placed this kind of police-work as a high priority. It may be reasonable to assume, therefore, that the comparably low priority to deal with the minor type of beat complaint influenced the volume of complaints to Becton police from the public because they felt that these reports would not be taken seriously. Other than the report of the elderly lady at Becton, I found no other evidence to indicate that residents did not complain to police because they were afraid that assailants would make the situation worse for the complainant. Estate Managers explained to me the action which could be taken by the council to help resolve such problems; in some instances the private patrol was directed to the problem area and asked by the Estate Manager to give the area some extra attention. In the example given above concerning the gypsy lady, it was said that after the private patrol attended the problem abated and the lady's problem had not recurred.

I decided to test the hypothesis that the private patrol were effectively influencing minor complaints on the Rams Estate. Research would discover the extent and quality of the patrols' effectiveness in these circumstances. After consulting Estate Managers and inspecting council records of the Rams Estate for a period of twelve months, I was able to identify several incidents in which the patrol may have been purposely diverted to deter some problem. These related to incidents of vandalism caused to the public areas of three blocks of flats; youths playing football in the inner corridors of a block of flats; harassment by youths of the gypsy woman; (as described above) threats of violence to a female tenant by an estranged boyfriend; domestic violence caused to a single female tenant by the father of her child; criminal damage by fire to storage areas in the basements of two blocks of flats and newly planted flower beds in the flats area destroyed by young vandals. I visited the scenes of each of these complaints and spoke to the complainants and those living nearby. I found that no one was aware of any positive effect which the patrol may have had upon the problems concerned and these problems continued to recur in most instances.

Patrols' influence on public disorder

Difficulties of definition and method were found in collecting the data in this particular area. Responses about how residents rated the patrol's ability to deter public disorder would not be influenced by their first hand experiences as there were no substantial public disorder problems at any of the research sites. Apart from Moston residents, who had prior to the start of the patrol experienced some minor street disorder, responses were based on imaginary impressions of how the patrol could control public disorder. I found that the free responses to this question were short and very vague and I attributed this to respondents' need to consider an imaginary situation. Typical responses were: 'Yes they would do a very good job', 'A good job', 'Quite good', 'No good' or 'Couldn't say'. I was unable to check if one individual's response was equivalent to another by asking for definitive examples to be given because of the inexperience of residents about such incidents. Although I adhered to the method of quantification adopted for the other interview data, (Oppenheim, op. cit.) due to the imaginary impressions of respondents, and the less meaningful content of their responses to this question, I found that the quantification of the data tended to be assigned more naturally to a five point coding frame which appears similar to a Likert scale (Likert, 1932). Accordingly, the legitimacy of the conclusions reached through use of this data must be considered in the light of these difficulties of definition and method.

As a public disorder deterrent the Becton patrol was seen as effective by 37 per cent of respondents while the Moston and Bridton patrols were seen as effective 52 per cent. There was no public disorder problem apparent at Moston. Any disorder had diminished with the installation of the patrol. Over half of those interviewed believed the patrol had effectively resolved their disorder problems and that it would not recur. Bridton residents saw the patrol as having the capacity to be similarly effective if required, yet public disorder had never been a problem for them.

Becton's absence of legitimacy

The Becton patrol's absence of 'authority' and their sheer non-presence were factors which influenced their ineffectiveness. For instance, at the flats where fire damage had occurred I asked the caretaker about the private patrol and he responded cynically:

> What patrol? I see the vans pass by, but very rarely. It is unusual to see them come into the blocks. They just drive by. I've seen them do nothing when children were jumping around on the low roofs. The children just follow them about and take the Mickey out of them. They never come and talk to me about problems.

Two typical responses from tenants of flats where damage was being caused further emphasised the ineffectiveness of the Becton patrol:

> Never seen them. They flash by in their vans but never come into the blocks. A kid was playing on a roof and he fell off and broke his arm. The security van was there. They just stood watching him. The kids do as they bloody well please. The security are shit. We were broken into but I didn't call the police. I found out who they were and they were given a good hiding. The old people on the top floor have been threatened. Let's see a couple of coppers around here. That's the answer.

> They drive in and drive off. There was once when one of their vans parked up outside my garage. It was still there twenty minutes later

when I wanted my car out. I went to the van and the guard was asleep inside.

The contract schedule, drawn up between Becton Council and the private agency, contained specific requirements for patrol functions. In the contract, 'calling the police' was one requirement. This implied positive action to be taken by patrol personnel. The fact that the council required such action would required the patrol to identify the offender for evidential purposes. This, in most cases, would require a confrontation between the offender and the patrolman. The instructions in the schedule, therefore, contained an additional, if only implied instruction, to do more than just call the police.

When it comes to the use of force private security personnel primarily derive what authority they have from those for whom they act as agents - private property owners. This authority exists in the contract between private security personnel and private persons - implied in which is the right of security operatives to remove, with reasonable force, trespassers from the 'private' property they are contracted to protect. When it comes to powers of arrest private security personnel have no additional power to that which we all have at Common Law - a citizen's power to arrest when it is reasonably believed that an arrestable offence has been committed or a breach of the peace is taking place. In R. v Podger (1979) and R. v Howell (1981) English law was clarified on arrest concerning a breach of the peace - which may be construed as not only public disorder but any criminal offence:

A private person or a constable may at common law arrest without warrant anyone who in his presence commits a breach of the peace where the offence is continuing, or if it is not continuing, where there is reasonable grounds for apprehending its renewal. A private person or a constable may also arrest without warrant anyone who there is reasonable ground to suppose is about to commit or about to renew a breach of the peace in his presence.

Williams (1979, p. 440) further clarifies the law on these matters concerning private persons. A person may use such force as is reasonable in the circumstances in the prevention of crime, or in effecting or assisting in the lawful arrest of offenders or suspected offenders or of persons unlawfully at large. These powers, which originally emanated in the Common Law, have now been incorporated into Section 24(2) of the Police and Criminal Evidence Act, 1984 which states:

Any person may arrest without warrant, (a) anyone who is in the act of committing an arrestable offence; (b) anyone whom he has reasonable grounds for suspecting to be committing such an offence.

As ordinary citizens, private security guards also have the right to self-defence and may use whatever reasonable force is required to protect themselves against attack. The legitimate use of force for private security guards is, accordingly, available but restricted. In this respect they are quite unlike the public police who are empowered by statute and the state with much broader powers of search, arrest and detention (Lustgarten, 1986, Chapters 1 and 2). Although Becton Council required positive action and confrontation by security guards with offenders, I found no evidence that the legitimate use of force they had available had been used in any incident they attended where arrest or other positive action could have been taken.

The function of reporting unlicensed vehicles on public roads is a traditional one for public police. I discovered that one of the Becton patrol's functions was to report these breaches to the local police. Since its inception the Becton patrol had not rigorously carried out this duty, however, I found that a newly installed security company were attempting to improve this record.

The difficult problem of legitimacy of force for the Becton patrol became apparent on one occasion when I was accompanying patrolmen on the Rams Estate. The patrol van was parked in a cul-de-sac next to a block of flats while I and a patrolman visited other nearby premises to check security. Another patrolman who was with us went to a nearby block to carry out similar checks. On our return to the van minutes later, we found that one of the tyres had been deliberately deflated. On discussing the reasoning behind this incident I was informed by a patrolman that the action had been retributive. Some days earlier the patrolman had discovered several unlicensed vehicles parked on a road nearby and he had reported the matter. While he had been recording details in the street the owner of the unlicensed vehicles appeared and an altercation occurred between him and the patrolman. Thus, the deflated tyre was attributed to the owner of the unlicensed vehicles. The patrolman told me he felt uncomfortable carrying out his duties on the estate:

My sister's afraid about me working here. I don't trust any of these people. If they shake your hand you are likely to walk away without some fingers.

Although the patrol's deterrent effect for public disorder was low at Becton, I found that some patrolmen talked positively about their effectiveness to deal with disorder. During my time spent patrolling with them, however, I found no support for these claims and no other evidence was forthcoming to confirm their views.

Function: prevention and assurance

The data presented here confirms the proactive, preventative, loss reductionist function of private security patrol (Reiss, 1983, 1987). This may be seen as further evidence of the traditional preventative nature of public policing being eroded by the private sector as they move into some areas of public police-work and blur the boundaries between the public and the private. One area, it is argued, is preventative patrol.

The recent history of preventative foot patrol in the British Police Service has more than an element of non-consistency concerning Home Office policy. This policy has moved from the idea of it being outmoded and uneconomic in the 1970's to its current fashionable position (Weatheritt, 1986, p. 23). An increase in recruiting over this time could be equated with the number of officers on foot, however, this is a simplistic assumption as research indicates otherwise. Brown and Iles (1985, pp. 52-53) show how beat officers are assigned to other duties away from their beats. They list ten separate reasons for this but identified 'paperwork' as the activity most likely to keep officers from foot patrol. This finding replicates the conclusions of earlier research that a large proportion of patrol officers' time is spent on administrative work, (Comrie and Kings, op. cit.) in particular report writing (Tarling and Burrows, 1983; Smith, 1983). This administrative burden has obviously increased tremendously with the introduction of legislation, such as The Police and Criminal Evidence Act and tape recording of interviews. It may not be surprising, therefore, to find that officers' time spent on the beat may have decreased. Such a situation will facilitate easier access by the private sector to traditional public policing.

Substantive evidence was found in the present research to demonstrate that private patrol allays the fear of crime (Donovan and Walsh, op. cit.). This finding, however, must be set against the 'updating process' which the private patrol used to educate residents about local problems. This process had the effect of perpetuating fear and insecurity.

When it comes to the legitimate use of force, however, no substantive evidence was found to support its use by private patrol. This tends to confirm the notion that matters which require resolving by legitimate force, such as arrest, usually remain the specific sovereignty of public police (Bittner, 1974).

The research in this section of the study has, again, clearly demonstrated the absence of a single perspective which can adequately explain the influences of change present at research sites. Rather, there is evidence both of emotional (Berger, Berger and Kellner, op. cit.; Giddens, 1981, 1984, 1991) and structural (Cohen, op. cit.) influences.

The Modus Operandi of protection

In this section I examine the means used by the patrol in providing protection. Data were collected by use of participant observation and official records. My research showed surveillance to be the primary method of protection (Shearing, Farnell and Stenning, 1981). I found that the surveillance used by the private patrol was directed at two separate targets, namely, potential offenders and clients of the security agencies.

Friend or foe?: offender surveillance

The ability to identify particular individuals or vehicles as 'friend' or 'foe' is crucial in differentiating between suspicious and non-suspicious incidents. Thus, local knowledge is an obvious asset in offender surveillance. Abstracts from the daily security logs of the Moston patrol showed the patrol's ability to identify suspicious incidents and recognize potential offenders. The local knowledge of the patrol personnel, at both Moston and Bridton, was apparent by their regular use of surnames associated with local criminal families. As I accompanied them on patrol they often identified persons seen, or merely brought into the conversation, as 'car thieves' or 'burglars' or generally 'troublemakers'. Patrol personnel were not only able to identify those who were a threat to the community, they had a special knowledge of the local residents. There were a number of occasions whilst accompanying patrol at Moston and Bridton that I became suspicious of certain persons and situations. Having pointed out the incident to the patrolman I was informed immediately of its innocent nature. Local knowledge is an obvious asset and comes naturally through regular street patrol. This local knowledge is the essence of community policing and has always been seen by the public police as the main attribute of the constable. As I observed the patrol personnel at Moston and Bridton I became aware of this part of their role as being analogous to that of the traditional constable.

During the period that I spent interviewing residents at Moston and Bridton I discovered it was impossible for me to be in these areas without being identified by duty patrol personnel. At subsequent meetings with them they always pointed out they had seen my car parked in the area, or a neighbour had told them I had visited. On each of the several evenings spent interviewing residents at Moston and Bridton I invariably came into contact with the patrol without prior arrangement. In contrast, during one week spent interviewing tenants on the Rams Estate at Becton I did not once make contact with the patrol.

Supervising carelessness: client surveillance

A considerable amount of patrol personnel spent time highlighting clients' negligent behaviour. Instances where patrolmen discover property left vulnerable and insecure required immediate action. If the client was available and the matter was serious enough the insecurity would normally be pointed out at the time. If the matter was discovered at an inconvenient time, for instance during sleeping hours, it became a matter of policy for the particular patrol what action they would take.

From abstracts of daily security logs at Moston the supervision of client-carelessness was clearly apparent. On discovering carelessness during late evening periods, however, the patrolmen at Moston were less likely to call people from their beds but instead gave extra attention to the vulnerable area throughout the night. Moston Security Services used their own letter-headed notepaper to inform clients of their carelessness. Matters of insecurity would be recorded on the notepaper and a copy delivered through the offending household's letter-box for later attention by the occupants - the 'snowflake' process (Shearing and Stenning, 1981, p. 215).

During my first meeting with Brian he listed some of the security problems he encountered on the Bridton patrol. They included, insecure windows and doors in houses garages and cars; keys left in the locks of houses garages and cars; handbags and purses left in cars; houses left unattended during darkness with all lights extinguished and curtains open; packages and parcels left on doorsteps; papers left in letter boxes and non-cancelled milk on the doorsteps of residents who were away on holiday. These forms of neglect of security were regularly monitored during patrol. Brian constantly spoke of his concern for clients' carelessness:

The job's about deterring, and you have to keep reminding them as well. Someone will come home with the shopping and have their hands full as they come in the door and forget to take the key out. That's the kind of thing I find. The other night a lady left her downstairs window open. I knocked her up and pointed it out. She got up and closed it.

My firsthand experiences patrolling alongside Brian confirmed his supervisory role. The monitoring entailed repetitive and monotonous checks as one house after another was examined for breaches of security. On going to the rear of one house Brian examined the security of the door and found it unlocked. He closed the door noisily telling me that these people often left the door insecure but, having reminded them with the 'slam', he knew they would lock it after we left. On another occasion Brian found a car insecure, called on the owners and pointed out their carelessness. They thanked Brian and assure him they would lock it. Early one morning Brian discovered a garage door insecure. The occupants were all in bed. Brian aroused them and pointed out the omission. An occupant of the house came downstairs and locked the garage.

Insecurities at Becton were evident in the patrol's maintenance reports, however, the direct contact which was maintained at Moston and Bridton with residents did not exist at Becton. I found no instances of residents' personal property being a particular concern to the Becton patrol. Insecurities, and other matters reported, related primarily to the council's responsibilities for their own property - not that of individual householders. Patrol reports mainly concerned the tower-block flats - where occupants were more economically deprived and owner-occupation was rare. These reports were forwarded directly to the council.

The essential nature of the private security patrol at all sites had a non-specialised character - as found in other research, responsibility for security fell to all concerned, not only the patrol personnel who are more likely to take on merely a supervisory role:

> Our survey of contract security guards indicated that, while they frequently engaged in such specialised security functions as controlling access to commercial facilities (26 per cent) they were employed mainly to supervise the performance of security functions by non-specialised personnel. (Shearing, Farnell and Stenning, 1980, p. 499).

Thus an important element of the security function was to check on clients to see they maintained a good level of security. Furthermore, this form of surveillance tends to be self induced and has a 'client defined mandate' (Shearing and Stenning, 1981, p. 209; Shearing and Stenning, 1983, p.498).

An invasion of privacy?

'Client' based surveillance at Moston and Bridton invaded occupants' privacy quite considerably. Surveillance at Moston was a relatively easy matter due to the layout of the area. Although the rear area of premises was surrounded by a high fence it was possible to see through it - giving an easy view of the state of security behind it. The patrol personnel at Moston had legitimate access to the outer areas of clients' property. Although close physical security of each residence was not carried out on a regular basis, clients' privacy was invaded by patrolmen who, from time to time, made close physical checks. This entailed making detailed examinations of windows and doors. In so doing, the opportunity was allowed for erosion of privacy through the various insight patrolmen gained into the private worlds of residents:

> We, in Britain, are only just beginning to appreciate the profound significance of the massive intrusion of private security into areas that were formerly the exclusive preserve of the police, as well as into areas of our lives which previously did not involve formal policing at all. (Slater, 1982b, p. 64).

Invasion of clients' privacy at Bridton was invariably more pronounced and on a more regular basis. A physical check of each client's property was carried out several times each day. All windows and doors were physically examined to ensure security. During the early occasions that I accompanied Brian I felt uncomfortable when invading residents' private space. Having gone into the rear garden of houses I was often confronted by the occupants, who were watching television or carrying out some domestic chore. Being accustomed to the patrol procedures they were not unnerved by our presence. As I accompanied the patrol more regularly my discomfort from these intrusions diminished somewhat, but not entirely. It was apparent, however, that residents did not find these intrusions objectionable. Several occasions were similarly presented which persuaded me that clients had forgone a considerable amount of privacy by contracting the patrol's services. However, they did not seem unduly concerned at this loss of privacy, indeed, in many instances its loss was being encouraged by them. During subsequent interviews I discovered that seeing the patrol about the neighbourhood was positively reassuring to residents. One client at Moston always left the curtains open no matter what the time of day. A patrolman told me:

They always leave them open. I sometimes think they're looking out for us so I make a point of walking past and letting them see me. It keeps them happy. It's what they like to see.

I did not find intrusion by the Becton patrol - its unobtrusive presence in terms of effectiveness has already been commented upon. Becton Council were sensitive to the possibility of intrusion. A survey of tenants conducted by the council in 1986 found that residents' privacy was not affected by the patrol's presence (Becton Council, 1987, pp. 2,6,12.). This finding tends to support the notion that Becton tenants, like those at Moston and Bridton, preferred, or at least did not object to, obtrusive surveillance.

Innocuous surveillance

Thus, the empirical evidence here clearly shows the nature of the surveillance used by the patrols had the capacity to be both pervasive and intrusive (Marx, op. cit., 1989; Kinsey, Lea and Young, op. cit.). It was not, however, pervasive in the same terms argued by these writers. With each target of surveillance - criminal or client - I found no evidence to show intrusion upon individual liberties in a coercive and sinister way. Indeed, to the contrary, there was evidence that 'client' surveillance was being encouraged by its subjects.

6 Relationships

In this chapter the study is focused upon the interrelationships which existed between the public and private police agencies at research sites. The effectiveness of the strategy to control crime is also examined.

Co-operation or confrontation?

The main aim in researching the public and private police relationships was to identify the proximity of the relationship so that conclusions could be drawn regarding its extent and quality. Factors of apparent organizational incompatibility, identified in the research of the U.S. Private Security Council (1977), were used in the interview schedule. Frequency and quality of liaison between the two agencies at each research site is measured and the level of threat to the professional status of the public police is identified. These three objectives were achieved partly through the use of observations and the examination of the work records of the private patrol and partly through interviews with police personnel. A semi-structured interview schedule was used with the police officers. In addition to unstructured conversation during the interview they were asked to respond to three structured value questions relating to some public/private relationships. It must be remembered that a given item may mean quite different things to different respondents and their responses, accordingly, may differ in meaning. These structured questions were not tested for such semantic differential. It is not methodically known, therefore, what level of uniformity existed among the respondents to the meaning of each item, or to the different response categories for each item. However, from my close working relationship and the long conversations I had with all the police officers, my impressions were that, especially at Bridton, very little semantic differential existed.

In order to ascertain the level of co-operative contact between the public and private agencies, public police officers were asked to state the number of times they had spoken to a private patrolman in the previous twelve months. Police officers are obliged to keep a minute by minute daily record of their duties and the incidents in which they become involved. For this purpose they keep an official note book. The recall data in this instance may be accepted as reliable because it was verifiable with the record kept in each officer's personal note book. My aim here was to record only those times when private and public officers came together operationally on patrol, 'in the field', rather than the less social, clinical setting of telephone contact. It was felt the best opportunity to identify occasions of co-operation existed at these times, when individuals met for a common purpose. My own experiences, as a patrolling police officer, and the experiences I had during this study supported the use of this method. I found that a high frequency of contact between public and private police existed at Bridton with less frequent contact at Moston. Very little contact occurred at Becton.

Moston   At Moston I ascertained that 23.5% of police officers had not come into contact with the patrol whatsoever and an equivalent number had only made contact up to five times in the previous twelve months. Significantly, only 17.6% contacted the patrol in excess of 50 times per year. Even if those occasions between 30-50 are added (11.8%) it cannot be claimed that the majority of the officers conferred with the patrol on a regular basis.

Bridton   The data obtained from questioning officers at Bridton showed that a high level of contact between the two agencies did exist. My observational study confirmed this finding. A police officer would visit Brian on at least one occasion during his daily period of duty and information was exchanged between them.

Becton   From subjective data there was no evidence of frequent conferences between the agencies at Becton. This finding was supported during my observations over the one month period that I carried out research on the Rams Estate. Indeed, I did not witness any meetings whatsoever.

The quality of contact and co-operation was examined through the subjective views of police officers and through observations during patrol time.

Moston   At Moston the majority of police officers interviewed believed the quality of co-operation to be 'average'. However, just under 30 per cent estimated co-operation to be either 'very good' or 'good' and none believed that 'bad' co-operation existed. During times that I accompanied the patrol I was present on a number of occasions when chance meetings between the two agencies occurred. These were used by both agencies to 'swap' information on local crime intelligence.

   During chance meetings between the police and the private patrol the police often asked private patrolmen to keep a lookout for stolen vehicles, or vehicles suspected to be used in crime. An example of the effectiveness of these meetings concerned such details being given to the patrol about a white Ford Sierra car being used locally for crime during early morning hours. Subsequently the Sierra was seen early one morning by the patrol and the information was immediately passed on to the police by use of a mobile telephone. The police responded promptly but unfortunately were unable to apprehend the occupants of the car.

   There were several other similar incidents which showed that good quality co-operation existed between the two agencies. This effectiveness was enhanced through radio and telephone communication between the police and the patrol. Important to the quality of this co-operation was the fact that patrol personnel were in possession of person to person radios and mobile telephones.

Bridton   All officers at Bridton believed co-operation to be very good. The area Sergeant explained the usual level of contact between the police and Brian:

> We do operate an unofficial liaison scheme and contact Brian every shift. He is well known by all local officers and is visited by us every night shift to keep in touch with what is going off. He resides in the area and is able to pass on to us good information about local criminals. He is likeable and trustworthy and hence the good liaison with the police. He is very conscientious and walks about in all weathers. He has been a Godsend to the Bridton area as his presence has certainly cut the crime rate. He has disturbed many people, some criminals, some not, and it is

well known that he walks the area. For any security service like this to work there must be a good liaison between them and the police.

I found that during the visits to Brian police officers would update him on local crime incidents and he would inform them of any suspicious individuals or vehicles he had seen on his patrol. The feeling amongst most local police officers was that while Brian was deterring crime on the estate it allowed them to get on with other business elsewhere.

Becton   There was no evidence of effective co-operation at Becton. The responses of the two police officers working on the Rams Estate sum up the relationship that existed between the police and the patrol:

> I have patrolled the Rams Estate in particular for six months but have had no contact with any private security on the estate at all.

> The other day I met a bloke from the patrol and we had a chat. I never met one of the patrolmen from the other company all the time they were here.

Threat

The level of threat to the professional status of the public police being posed by the private security patrol was measured. This was achieved by interviewing police officers and ascertaining their concern. In general terms the response to this question showed how public police saw the private patrol as 'non-threatening' to their professional status.

Moston   If police accept the usefulness of better domestic locks and alarms, the role of private security transporting money and the notion of better co-operation between neighbours to make crime more difficult for the criminal, then why should police object if private citizens pay a security firm to keep an eye on their homes and cars? Some would see this reaction by the police as concerning a threat to state power (Boostrom and Henderson, op. cit., p. 28). In this view, citizens can expect to experience resistance from public police who see their legitimacy as being challenged.

If rank and file police officers at Moston felt no threat from the private patrol some senior police officers had a different view. In particular, the Chief Constable strongly objected to the implementation of private patrols. The views of the Chief Inspector at Moston reflected this policy. In contrast to my findings, he assured me that the liaison between the two agencies was not good. The feeling of disharmony, which the Chief Constable and the Police Committee had towards the scheme, is further shown in local newspaper reports concerning the introduction of private security patrol in the area. No official liaison existed between the police and private security at Moston. Indeed the Police Committee had made it clear there was to be none. The Committee also called upon the Chief Constable to investigate the operations of Moston Security Services for they strongly opposed 'vigilante' patrols and they would not tolerate them in the region.

The views of the Chief Constable and his Police Committee had affected Moston residents' attitude to the public police. This became immediately clear to me on the first occasion that I visited the estate. In company with one of the private patrolmen I introduced myself as a police officer to one of the residents. After being invited into the house the lady told me she would not have let me in if I had not been in company with the private patrolman. This theme was repeated later by other residents who I interviewed. The reasoning for this attitude, they told me, was because as the private scheme was introduced there was a flurry of media interest which was precipitated by the Chief Constable's open approach to media coverage. This, coupled with his aversion to private security patrol helped focus attention upon the Moston residents. Thereafter their privacy was penetrated by the arrival of the press. This had made them very sensitive towards the press and the police. The owner of Moston Security Services had briefed me on residents' sensitivity to these matters. He too had been harassed by the press. Reporters from BBC television had suggested that he and the Chief Constable should take part in a debate to be broadcast on national television. Due to residents' sensitivity to this matter I began to doubt whether I would be allowed access to the data which they could provide through interviews.

In order to legitimize my access into this sensitive situation I found it necessary to ask the owner of Moston Security Services to meet residents and attempt to persuade them that I had their best interests at heart. Fortunately he was able to do this successfully and I was able to continue interviews unhindered.

Bridton   I found no evidence that police saw the Bridton patrol as a threat to their profession.

Becton   In respect of their professional status the officers at Becton did not feel threatened by the patrol. Although no liaison existed at Becton I nevertheless found no unwillingness by the police to accept the role of the private agency.

Co-operation not confrontation

The data collected at Moston and Bridton provides evidence that regular and high quality co-operation existed between the private patrol and the police. Thus, co-operation between the private patrol and the police was clearly providing a net increase on the quantity and quality of surveillance in the area (Shearing and Stenning, 1981, pp. 213-214). This was so even though within the public police organization at Moston a contradiction existed between policy-makers and those operational officers putting it into practice. Contrary to the apparent confrontation between public and private agencies, seen in policy statements by the Police Committee and senior police management, good working relationships did exist. At Bridton no such complicated process existed and relationships were clearly very close and cooperative. In contrast to Moston and Bridton there was little contact evident between the agencies at Becton. But what little evidence did exist at Becton indicated a willingness by the public police to legitimize the operations of private security.

Some Chief Constables have indicated their approval of the private security industry in crime prevention (Anderton, 1982; Newman, 1985). The notion that better relations with the public, including private security, will increase the flow of criminal intelligence (Alderson, 1982) is now a central part of Home Office and police strategy. Community policing and neighbourhood watch schemes embrace this concept. The flow of information from public to police is crucial in detection, for it is the public who influence this the most (Greenwood, Chaiken and Petersilia, 1977; Burrows and Tarling, 1987; Bottomley and Coleman, op. cit.). Improved liaison between the police and private security, coupled with the positive reaction of Chief Officers, would appear to be an important factor in the effective flow of information to the police (Skolnick and Bayley, 1986).

If surveillance by private security patrol in residential areas can be seen as successful then the implementation of innovative public policies providing a fairer distribution of protection may be welcome. The most successful ingredients for institutional innovation in inter-agency co-operation need therefore, to be identified. What is most important in this respect is Chief Officers' genuine commitment to the values of a crime prevention-orientated police force (Skolnick and Bayley, ibid.) and the enhancement of inter-organizational relationships by 'Boundary Spanning' (Leifer and Delbecq, op. cit., pp. 40-41). 'Boundary Spanners' are persons who operate at the periphery of an organization and carry out functions relating to its environment. The degree to which the organization's boundaries are open and receptive to inputs is crucial to its survival and effectiveness (Leifer and Delbecq, op. cit.; Johnson, 1972, 1976; Keller, 1978).

The fact that empirical findings in this part of the study show there to be a high degree of co-operation between public and private agencies (Slater, op. cit.) creates a persuasive tendency to describe a Janus-faced state, standing central and scanning on the apparent boundary between the public and the private (Cohen, 1979, 1985). But the interpretation here is not one as sinister as Cohen (ibid.) would have us believe - for it would be remiss not to recognize the positive effects that increased surveillance may have on the prevention and detection of crime. Yet, there is still a negative aspect to this strategy. Although there appears to be no clear institutional boundary between the public and the private this is not of great concern here - other than to note the fact that the state is neither wholly public nor private, corporate or welfare (Unger, 1976). What is of concern, however, is the way that the strategy functions. It is important to understand that it functions in selected areas of economic stability and, thus, it has a tendency to function for the economically liberated and keeps in mind the economically subdued as a target for its function. There is just the possibility that such strategies may be seen as ideological devices of the state (Althusser, 1971, pp. 137-138).

7 Crime control

In this chapter the levels of crime that exist within the research sites are examined. An attempt is made thereafter to identify any effect patrol may have upon incidence and distribution of crime. Using a crime pattern analysis of data collected from police registers, a conclusion is presented which considers not only the benefits of enhanced protection but also disadvantages of the strategy.

A crime-pattern analysis

Moston

Moston residents were convinced that the patrol had reduced local crime. Having interviewed residents about the scheme a local newspaper reporter summed up their claims:

> Since they called in a private security firm to patrol their streets at night Moston residents claim that regular car and home break-ins have become a thing of the past. (The private security patrol).......has worked extremely well and everyone thinks it is marvellous because the youths who were hanging about causing trouble have been scared off and the number of incidents have gone down notably. (Newcastle Journal, 1988).

To further examine the accuracy of these subjective claims I abstracted recorded crime for the period between 1986 and 1989 from the records of the Moston Police. Using this data, a bivariate, longitudinal analysis was made between the patrolled area and an un-patrolled area nearby. The un-patrolled area, situated approximately fifty yards from the patrolled area, consists of thirty one high quality, owner-occupied houses and bungalows. On average the market price of housing on the un-patrolled area is £5,000 cheaper than on the patrolled site. Although both sites are of a high standard of appearance the un-patrolled site is slightly less tidy than the other. Residents in the un-patrolled area are mainly professional and white collar workers. It is reasonable, however, to describe both areas as similar in geographical, structural and socio-economic terms.

Some conclusions can be drawn on the 'before' and 'after' effects of the patrol at Moston. These should, however, be seen in the light of the small number of offences recorded which make it imprudent to comment with certainty. Nevertheless, there was an overall fall in crimes reported in 1989 on the patrolled area and no similar decrease on the un-patrolled area. It would not be unreasonable to interpret this contrast as 'deflecting' crime into the neighbouring un-patrolled area.

The temporal analysis of crime at Moston could not identify any pattern to show that crime was occurring more during a particular period of the day. This is usually the consequence of complainants discovering they are the victims of crime on some occasion long after it occurred - for instance on returning home after several days away and discovering a burglary. In these instances it is often impossible to know the time or day when the offence took place. The data collected, therefore, was not representative of the complete picture of when offences were taking place and its value must be considered accordingly. Limited data did, however, show that most crime occurred between 6pm and 6am - when the patrol was on duty. This has to be seen in relation to the fact that the Moston patrol visited periodically - security guards' visits were made in between visits to the nearby industrial estates. Although there was no evidence to show that those carrying out the crimes waited for the departure of the patrol before doing so this is a possible consideration. Because of the small size of the Moston estate, however, it was very apparent if the patrol was present or not. It would seem unlikely, therefore, that criminals needed to watch for the patrol's departure as they could immediately see at a glance if the patrol were there or not.

Bridton

Using police records a similar comparison to that made at Moston was made at Bridton. In this case sufficient data was available to safely legitimize conclusions. Before considering this data it is important to show whether or

111

not it was consistent with the general crime trend in a wider geographical area. For this purpose five categories of crime were considered from within the police section wherein the Bridton Estate is located.

A decrease in the general crime rate in the Bridton area had occurred between 1988 and 1989. Apart from the category of vehicle crime this was fairly consistent with the recorded crime on the specific areas of patrol and non-patrol. The data has been incorporated into a bar-chart, Figure 7.1 which presents a striking view of the contrasting crime rates in the patrolled and un-patrolled areas.

A general decline in overall reported crime can be seen on the patrolled area. In contrast, crime on the un-patrolled area increased in 1988 and 1989 after maintaining relative constancy in previous years. This general finding is evident in the two dominant reported crime categories of burglary and theft. All burglaries reported were from dwelling houses. The category 'theft' is divided into 'theft of and from vehicles' and 'all other theft'. It can be seen that the former category is by far the most commonly reported crime. This is important to note, given the extent of vehicle possession on the estate and the easy opportunity for offenders to participate in this type of crime.

Burglary Burglaries reported in 1986 reflected the upward trend in overall crime on the estate that year, especially in the patrolled area which shows a comparative increase with the un-patrolled area of the estate (25:16). This illustration represents the period of concern which residents experienced prior to hiring the patrol. By the end of 1987, however, the gap between the comparative areas was closing, although burglary in the un-patrolled area was still less than the patrolled section but only slightly less. (11:8). By 1988 the trend had reversed. (2:13) and continued in 1989 (2:6). This is a significant finding in respect of the patrol's deterrent ability. Furthermore, burglary in dwellings recorded on the whole of the police section showed a sharp decrease from 1988 to 1989 and this corresponds with a decrease of nearly 50 per cent in the un-patrolled area. In contrast, recorded burglary in the patrolled area remained constant.

Theft (other) In this category the un-patrolled area maintained a constant rate in 1984 and 1985 increasing only slightly in 1986. However, in common with other crime variables during that year, (burglary and theft of and from vehicles), the patrolled area showed a comparative increase of about 50 per cent. Once again, by 1987 the patrolled area was beginning to show decreases in comparison with the un-patrolled area of the estate. This remained constant for the next three years.

Total Crime Recorded

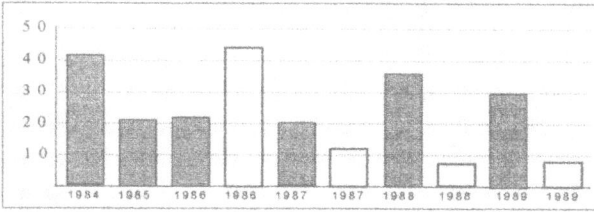

Burglary

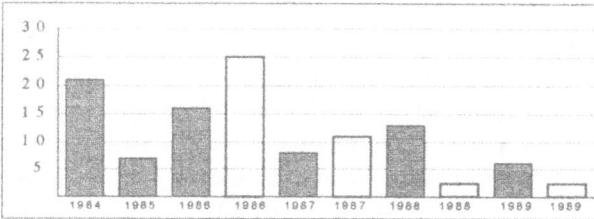

Theft (other)

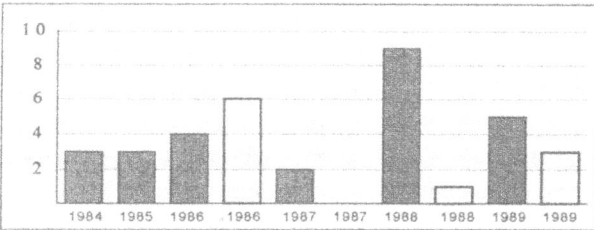

Theft (of/from vehicles)

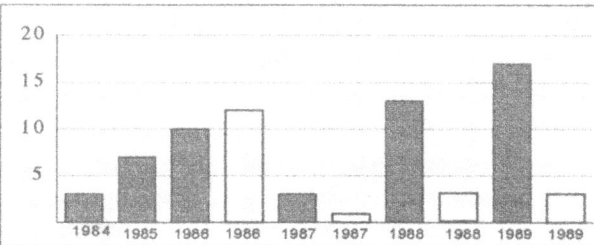

☐ Patrolled   ■ Un-patrolled

Figure 7.1   Comparative annual crime rate at Bridton

113

Other than in 1987, the un-patrolled area saw an increase in this category of offence for each year. From 1986 the patrolled area recorded a significant decrease until 1989. 1986 had again been a year when the patrolled area's crime had exceeded that of the un-patrolled area. There are particularly wide ratios between the two areas in 1988 and 1989 (3:13; 3:17). Furthermore, whereas the un-patrolled area showed an increase in offences from 1988 to 1989, the patrolled area remained low and constant. The increase in the overall police section crime between 1988 and 1989 corresponded with an increase in the un-patrolled area. There is an important significance in the above comparisons between the overall police section crime and the two controlled areas. This relates to theft of and from motor vehicles which, in contrast to the two other categories of offence, increased both at section level and in the un-patrolled area yet decreased in the patrolled area.

The distribution by time of offences at Bridton was a similar pattern to Moston. Most crime occurred during the 6pm - 6am period on both the patrolled and un-patrolled areas. The fact that offences still occurred during the presence of the patrol reminded me that total security is likely to be unachievable - no matter what is put in the way of the committed criminal he can evade it if he is determined enough.

Some conclusions can be drawn on the 'before' and 'after' effects of the patrol. These should, however, be seen in the light of the small number of offences recorded. Nevertheless, there does appear to be an overall fall in crimes reported on the patrolled area and no similar decrease on the un-patrolled area. It would not be unreasonable to interpret this contrast as 'deflecting' crime into the neighbouring un-patrolled area.

Becton

It would be unrealistic to believe that the deterrent ability of eight men in four vans patrolling an area the size of Becton (60 square kilometres) could be quantified with any legitimacy using data from police records. Such small fish in a large sea are not likely to have noticeable effects upon the distribution of crime. In view of this, no crime pattern analysis was attempted at Becton. Instead, some general references are made to data collected during the research. Confirming its impotency, a council policy officer who had worked on the introduction of the patrol pilot scheme at Becton told me:

It was obviously going to have little effect in the large area it had to cover. The follow-up research on its effectiveness was inconclusive but the patrol was retained nevertheless.

The leader of the Federation of Becton Council Tenants described the effectiveness of the patrol as symbolic rather than practical:

> It worked. It acted as a deterrent at first but once the youngsters found out how far they could go with the security men it began to deteriorate. But it still did have a function. It did more for the local tenants in having another presence around their property. It was well worth the costing. I have no doubt that the patrol was set up from the basis of the tenants' arguments.

A senior research officer, previously employed by the council at the inception of the patrol and whose research had been instrumental in council decisions to begin the patrol, described reservations about the project:

> I found that when they got started they needed constant supervision to be effective and it was impossible. The large area that such a small number had to cover, and the number of jobs they were expected to carry out, meant that their effectiveness was doubtful. It was really a sop.

A more orthodox version of the policy implementation process was described by the principal officer in charge of the research department at the time:

> The conclusion reached was that it was a good idea but there were several things which were not happening. The security guards were not using their common-law power of arrest. Once the locals knew this they took advantage of the guards. We found it hard to assess whether we were getting value for money or not. This kind of patrol is about symbolism and its difficult to quantify.

There is an important factor to note from this and previous data concerning the effectiveness of the Becton patrol. Although the patrol was clearly functionally impotent the council still maintained that it should continue to operate. This tends to confirm the finding described earlier that the patrol was literally symbolic in terms of the council's need to appear to be enhancing the public good.

The ethics of crime displacement

The result of the crime pattern analysis illustrates clearly a contrast in levels of burglary and theft between the patrolled and un-patrolled areas, especially marked at Bridton. The significantly lower rate in the patrolled area, which cannot be accounted for by mere environmental or economic differences alone, may reasonably be seen in relation to the enhanced surveillance prevailing. The temporal analysis, which indicated that crime continued to occur during the operational times of the patrol, was evidence of the determination of some offenders. It is argued, however, that this fact hardly affects the analysis of displacement of crime because the 'determination' factor in some offenders will always exist. The temporal findings are likely, therefore, to be common to most research of this type and, although an extraneous factor, it does not weaken the argument for displacement. This argument is particularly supported by the strong difference in the rate of theft of, and from vehicles - crimes which require the offender to place himself in clearly observable positions. Protective cover for the offender during this offence is less possible than during burglary. Theft of, and from vehicles, therefore, apparently lends itself well to detection by patrolling personnel. Indeed, 'visibility to those nearby' is an important consideration to those committing crime in residential areas (Reppetto, op. cit.).

The theory of rational choice is therefore of importance to the crime patterns identified at Moston and Bridton. Both areas of the estates, whether patrolled or un-patrolled, share similar profiles in respect of availability, 'likely cash yield', 'cover', and so on. An important and crucial difference, however, was the risk of identification or apprehension by the enhanced surveillance in the patrolled areas. According to rational choice theory this difference, together with the social and economic uniformity of both areas, is likely to create displacement (Cornish and Clarke, 1988).

This part of the research has shown that, at Moston and Bridton, offenders' conscious decisions about the location of likely success correlates with crime levels. In view of this, the successful manipulation of the environment by enhanced patrol may well account for most of the variation in levels and distribution of crime. Thus there is support for the notion that the unethical effects of 'displacement' correlate with private security patrol in neighbourhoods and the crime policy of neo-conservatives and the Home Office.

8 Conclusions and policy implications

The contribution the research has made to the area of study is demonstrated in this chapter by drawing attention to why, and in what ways, neighbourhood private security patrol differs or concurs with the notion of sinister, disciplinary and oppressive policing. The empirical findings are also analysed in respect of the notion that ineffective public policing leads to the demand for private security patrol. A general analysis of the fieldwork is also made with reference to socio-legal and police studies. As the primary findings are scattered throughout the preceding text it will be helpful to restate and analyse them through the use of the six key concepts which have been referred to throughout the thesis.

Motivation: an agent and structure partnership

At Moston and Bridton the motive for hiring private security patrol contained a strong element of human agency which was supported by state policy of market enterprise in security provision - self-help and choice. The existence of agency was demonstrated by the comparative freedom and autonomy with which residents could act to hire private patrol. However, although it was evident that self-help and choice were important principles of state policy to Moston and Bridton residents, their concern at increased crime and disorder was emotionally influenced to a greater degree than the residents at Becton. At Becton it was apparent that an important aspect of the council's management style was to promote entrepreneurship and to seriously espouse government principles of self-help and choice. Although the Federation of Becton Council Tenants had a degree of influence upon the decision to contract-in private security, Becton Council saw it as part of a crusade to promote private enterprise at any cost.

Thus, in this part of the study, it can be seen that motivation to hire private security patrol consisted of both structural (state policy on policing provision) and agency influences. The thesis propounded by some left-functionalists, that involuntary human/state relationships exist, cannot therefore, be supported by the empirical findings. They do support the claim, however, that left-functionalism underestimates the autonomy of individual self-interest (Berger, Berger and Kellner, op. cit.; Ignatieff, op. cit.; Giddens, 1984). There is specific empirical illustration in this part of the study to support a theory of structuration (Giddens, ibid.). In such a theory the mutual dependency, rather than opposition, of human agency and social structure is emphasised. Social structures are intimately involved in the production of action and are not seen as restricting and repressive of individual action. It is the structural properties of social systems which provide the means by which people can act.

The particular notion that the instigation of private security patrol can be associated with ineffective public policing is now considered in relation to the empirical findings.

The scientific management of policing:
the police service as a business

Freedom of choice and self-help have become institutions of policing. As the state becomes increasingly unable to provide sufficient services for individual and corporate protection so individuals begin depending upon private forms of policing. The management of danger through prevention in everyday life is now primarily a matter for informal crime prevention strategies such as private security patrol. When demand drives the available services into scarcity the market begins to look for substitution or alternative, less expensive services. This search leads to new options for both individuals and state institutions.

Private security patrol, therefore, bridges the gap between public expectations of security services and the existing reality of police protection. It develops, as identified in this study, because of a feeling that the police are ineffective in performing services essential to a stable community (Marx and Archer, 1971, p. 57; Slater, 1982a, p. 19; Slynn, op. cit.; Albanese, op. cit., p. 86; Wildeman, 1988). Respondents' views of police ability to provide adequate protection at Moston and Bridton clearly showed that they saw policing inadequacies. Although that feeling at Becton was not quite so pronounced, the majority of respondents, nevertheless, felt a similar inadequacy existed. This slight variance of feeling between Moston/Bridton and Becton residents may be seen as reflecting Becton Council's influence in promoting the use of the private patrol upon an area whose inhabitants, although dissatisfied with public police provision, were relatively content with the service they were receiving.

An extensive and influential report on efficiency in the police service notes that Home Office policies of value for money and cost effectiveness have dramatically influenced traditional expectations of public policing, affecting the wide discretional powers officers on the beat previously enjoyed (Operational Policing Review, op. cit.). Furthermore, the quality of police work now depends in part upon strategies of capital controlled within highly bureaucratic systems (Rowe, 1986, pp. 67-68). The traditional form of police professionalism has been subordinated to bureaucratic control where both the client can assert control and the state can mediate between client and profession and, accordingly, control the conditions of their relations (Johnson, 1972, 1976). This idea of making better use of labour power through scientific management has penetrated traditional policing and is a contributing factor to the introduction of private forms of police (Spitzer and Scull, 1977b, p. 25). The policy document most associated with this contemporary change in police management (Home Office, 1983) marked a further move away from the managerial style which emphasised actions rather than results. The pressure of cost, together with rising crime, was being used to demand effective action from the police. Chief Constables and Police Authorities would need to have clear ideas on objectives and priorities (Home Office, ibid., pp. 1-3). The primary strategy they would encourage and implement was self-help policing in the community. Senior police officers have argued that these Home Office demands for effectiveness and efficiency have resulted in what has been empirically illustrated in this study - a reduction in the presence of uniform officers on the streets, a decline in the perceived services to the public and consequently an increase in the growth of private security patrols in residential areas (Hilliard, 1989, p. 2028).

When it comes to neighbourhood policing individuals are motivated by a need for a level of security which enables them to exist with the least possible anxiety. Individuals need continuity and order in events (Giddens, 1991, Chapter 7) for our desire for security emerges early in life and is as important to us as impulses of thirst and hunger (Sullivan, 1953, p. 14). This ontological security is an associate motivator with state policy on public choice and self-help. Thus, the private vigorously emerges through a dual process of state policy and human emotion. But self-help and choice are more likely to allude economically underprivileged individuals. It is the better-off in society who are able to fully satisfy the ontological aspects of security.

Exclusive communities

Privatization of police work is associated with community insularity and isolation, paranoia and prejudice (Suttles, op. cit.; Pitkin, op. cit., p. 327). Deviance boundaries are redrawn as communities take measures to protect themselves. As the problem of who to blame for the crime problem is localized in an alien culture the exclusive community feels safer as a result. Disruption in community solidarity increases repressive justice (Erikson, 1966) as individuals, independent of their actions, become increasingly repressed following an external threat to the entire social system (Cohen, 1985). A siege mentality is created.

It is argued here that the findings are not suggestive of a general trend in social control moving from secondary towards primary relations, as some left-functionalists argue (Melossi, 1979; Mathiesen, op. cit.) but that there exists a trend away from community spirit towards active individualism and inactive collectivism. There is a disengagement of individuals from collectives and these communities tend to shun and are suspicious of the state. Far from practising self-help most people do not participate in activities outside the immediate family.

Instead of planning for order and control the left-functionalist approach argues that the plan should be for human happiness and fulfilment (Cohen, ibid., pp. 264-267). It is difficult, however, to see how this argument is a helpful one because if moving towards a socialist transformation would reduce sinister surveillance one wonders what becomes of the inevitable need for individual security inherent in us all. Another paradox of this argument is that social control should be located in the community - the very master move seen as the epitome of capitalism's crisis.

Function

While there is support for the notion of a socio-economic and political rationale in the motivation for private patrols, another central factor concerns individual's fear of crime (Donovan and Walsh, op. cit.) - clearly allayed by this strategy. But patrol's overall usefulness in this area is limited due to the small and almost exclusively middle-class areas it services. Furthermore, as found in this study, private security patrol tends to be bound up with a self-fulfilling prophecy. For as patrol personnel carry out their daily interactions with those around them, they may perpetuate fear by deflecting it back to their clients during their conversations about local crime (Skogan and Maxfield, op. cit.; Garofalo, op. cit.; Greenberg, Rohe and Williams, op. cit.; Rosenbaum, op. cit.). In this respect it could be argued that private security patrol has the capacity to strengthen the state's control of the whole community (Cohen, op. cit.).

Security as symbolic

Individual's basic need for security is often a non-quantifiable element of policing provision. The problem with security is that it is difficult to define as a commodity - primarily defined in negative terms it exists when something does not occur rather than when it does. Described as 'sound' and 'calculated', its function is based on faith in the predictable in an unpredictable world (Spitzer, 1987, p. 47). Thus a constant uncertainty exists (Berman, 1982) which is substantially resolved by opting for the choice of the symbolic, unquantifiable nature of security provision. These are important factors, for they are the essence of the symbolic nature of policing.

Purely structural\functional arguments concerning security tend to attention from the crucial analysis of security, as seen in this and the other empirical studies mentioned above - security as symbolic, social and intangible. Here the present study could be interpreted as the rationalization of social life through choice - a strategy to meet the social, political and economic problems inherent in contemporary public policing. An historical moment of crises now exists and a particular form of policing is created to coincide with the particular capitalist strategy designed to meet the crisis. This crisis management strategy - self-help surveillance and choice - functions in reality through the market, wherein subjective fears and desires can be directed through the social institution (Spitzer, ibid., p. 58).

Although Spitzer's analysis of consciousness is commendable, it is based upon consciousness as ideology or superstructure and as such it is a dependent variable of infrastructures of domination. The empirical findings of the present study cannot be interpreted that way as it would not allow consciousness to be dealt with on its own terms - for the situation of contemporary life and thought is shaped not only by external forces of modernity but by the forces of modern consciousness, which bring attention to the importance of ontological security. And it is precisely at this point of theoretical departure that the perception of individual action may be assessed as social rather than economic. The strategy of private security patrol is not a purely structural phenomenon where infrastructures of domination are imposed upon the social. It is not simply created by capitalist relations of production. It is clearly influenced by generic features of industrial societies, which includes consciousness (Saks, 1983, pp. 1-21). So, although such strategies depend upon the mobilization of purely structural aspects of state approval (Home Office, 1979, 1983) they also depend upon the willingness of populations to look for expert help, especially in times of 'security crisis'.

Surveillance and control

Although detection and subsequent disciplinary forms of punishment are not totally dismissed in opportunity-reduction, this form of policing is concerned primarily to prevent crime than to apprehend offenders. Social control, therefore, appears to lie elsewhere than in the disciplinary area of the punishment system. Such a non-disciplinary system, concerned as it is with consequences as opposed to fault, seeks primarily to regulate activity (Kamenka and Tay, 1975). In that type of regulatory system, as found in the present study, it is possible for individuals to be 'active participants and 'passive receivers' of social control at their own behest. Thus, it cannot always be argued that subordination exists and that control is merely obtained through coercive state surveillance.

This analysis relies crucially upon the distinction between juridical penality and disciplinary (carceral) penality (Bottoms, 1983, p. 196). It is important to carefully analyse particular features of surveillance before differentiation can be made. Bottoms (ibid., p. 177) describes a model based upon the analysis of power by Foucault (op. cit., pp. 130-131) and identifies the central features of corporal, juridical and carceral mechanisms of punishment. Using that model it is possible to identify the two forms of surveillance in the present study, 'client' and 'offender'. Foucault's disciplinary effect is obtained directly through 'training' mechanisms which require knowledge of the offender's whole person. In the present study, however, there is no need for this sinister and personally penetrating disciplinary form of punishment - a more juridical form of punishment predominates.

The strategy of surveillance in private security patrol is concerned more with prevention than apprehension. Control tends primarily to exist outside the disciplinary area of the punishment system and focuses on consequence not fault. There exists, nevertheless, the possibility for individuals to be both active and passive actors in this system. Control, therefore, cannot just be seen as a coercive state mechanism - it must be seen as a reflexive response to individuals (Berger, Berger and Kellner, op. cit.; Giddens, 1979, 1984, 1991).

Co-operation

In terms of the traditional preventative aspect of policing, the study has demonstrated support for the notion that clear distinctions do not exist between public and private agencies. This is because public police administrators, whether at the Home Office or more parochially located, are seeking to achieve inter-agency co-operation in many ways. In this respect, police administrators 'scan' (Leifer and Delbecq, op. cit.) to bolster depleted public police manpower (O'Connor, op. cit.). In terms of power, at Bridton especially, there was some evidence of the public police seeking to attain its goals at the expense of the private agency (Schmidt and Kochan, op. cit., p. 220). Nevertheless, the degree of genuine co-operation between the two agencies was found to be high. This requires an appraisal of the idea of 'police'.

Police: a less limited notion

Police are so much in our everyday lives that most of us believe we know what 'the police' as an institution is. So often our perceptions are influences by the media who compound rigid images. Likewise, the Oxford Dictionary restricts the idea of police to 'Civil administration, public order, department of government concerned with this....'. Similarly, the term has been used to describe persons with a special legal status who are employed by governments to keep the peace (Parks, 1970). These descriptions carry with them connotations of merely government control and authority (Shearing, Farnell and Stenning, 1980, p. 17).

Since the implementation of the New Police in 1829 policing services have indeed been dominated by state provision. Yet the origins of contemporary public policing have been examined against a notion of a public peace which is said to have its origins in a multiplicity of private peace's going back to antiquity (Keeton, 1975). The single public peace, emanating from the time of the New Police, is the Sovereign's peace and has been described as devouring competing private peace's (Maitland, 1913, p. 108). This historical epoch saw the birth of the nation-state; a public authority which dominated all other authorities but which allowed private liberties. But although in modern times there appears to be a dominant public peace there is still no satisfactorily clear distinction between the public and the private (Becker, 1973).

The apparently dominant, and in inaccurate, perception of clear distinctions may be sinister in its self for it can be argued that within public police organizations limited notions of definition can be used as political forces to ensure organizational survival. Thus 'the' Police have been seen as adopting their own protective mandate and myth and manipulating public expectations (Manning, 1977, p. 38). From this standpoint Britain's police, and policing as a general concept, exists in a limited universe which consists merely of the membership of the Police Federation of England and Wales and other police representative bodies within the public sector. This creates a problem for policing equity, for there is a tendency to become trapped at an institutional level of analysis upon which there is no room for an ever-growing private sector police and their particular function. One only has to read the Police Federation's magazine, 'Police' to find proof of their negative approach towards private security. This view of private security as having no place in traditional policing functions is also taken strongly by a great many senior police officers. Thus, it would appear that the public police would wish the existence of inter-agency co-operation, but only on their terms.

Public and private: one entity

In ancient societies public and private states were not so fixed as they appear today. Extended family systems were deeply integrated so that behaviour was constantly under surveillance. To conceive of oneself as having a separate identity from the neighbourhood would have been difficult in those times. The private emerged as a social conception when individuals separate themselves from the locality and created social distance. Public officials, often guarantors of public morality, are of course private individuals too. The state must contain, therefore, both public and private elements (Bensman and Lilienfeld, 1979, p. 173). The boundaries of the state are constantly shifting and cannot be categorized as either welfare or corporate - a welfare-corporate state exists (Unger, op. cit.). State power is, therefore, very much a question of the extent to which the aspect of centralised juridico-political ordering dominates over others that might be in play at any given time (Nowell-Smith, 1980, p. 9). And this has an important bearing on policy implications for this study. For as a concept this 'fluid' state has potential to allow change in justice systems. Such change is most likely to occur where state power is unchallenged, where criminality directed at private persons is perceived to be a serious and increasing threat and where ideology does not preclude private security (Bayley, 1986, p. 51).

The findings in the present study fit well with the notions of policing discussed above. Public policing, accordingly, will never permanently replace private policing. Private security policing has a political relationship with the state and may become dominant in some areas of police work. This exclusion of a strict definitive division of function between public and private agencies allows in the notion that the Home Office is at one and the same time the master of public and private policing. In such an environment of co-operation, delegation and diversion, the shedding of the soft-end of policing is assisted. Thus the state can get on with the more serious aspects of crime (Cohen, op. cit., p. 138). Currently, what appears at first sight to be minimal statism is in fact increased statism as the Home Office maintain the power to influence criminal justice policy towards an increasing corporate level and, consequently, also influence patterns of crime.

Crime control

Neighbourhood private security patrol has the capacity to be effective in preventing crime, however, there is evidence here to argue a mistaken belief in crime prevention. Crime was deflected, not necessarily prevented. Although it may not be politically acceptable to neo-conservatives crime deflection is a more appropriate term to use here. Accordingly, choices of policy made at an institutional level (Home Office) and choices of practice individual security purchasers) create crime patterns. Crime deflection has been identified here as part of a larger framework where the distribution of crimes and their victims is the result of a series of choices taken by certain sections of society. This is a valuable part of the study because it identifies how, when choices are taken, crime patterns occur.

While the state encourages individuals to purchase their own security (Home Office, 1989) it is worth remembering that not everyone can respond positively to this message - for not everyone has the economic power, or the will, to purchase security. Large areas of society do not have the power of choice. Increased security measures are, therefore, a good thing for those exclusive communities who have purchased them. Those who have not, for instance, those who do not have private security patrol, should not be surprised if they experience more of the crime problems that their better patrolled neighbours formerly experienced but now deflect elsewhere. Accordingly, inequality leads to oppression.

An oppressive juridical mechanism

The theoretical analysis here does not proceed from the notion of a repressive state discipline obtained by training mechanisms requiring knowledge of the offender's whole person (Foucault, op. cit.). More appropriately, the analysis must begin from a position which considers juridical punishment as a primary factor. Private security patrol in neighbourhoods relies more on a bureaucratic-administrative type of regulation backed up by a Gesellschaft type penality. This form of control is achieved through the attainment of goals and norms (Kamenka and Tay, op. cit. p. 138), directed at whole groups and categories of people (Mathiesen, op. cit.) and operated often by the people themselves (Shearing and Stenning, 1983, p. 488, 1987b). Indeed, as Smart (1983) points out, Foucault himself propounded the notion that discipline is decreasing as a control technique and that a more normative, regulatory and juridical style of control is developing in the community (Foucault, 1979b, p. 139). In the present study this style of control has been formalized. The informal control characteristic, normally associated with the small homogeneous primary communities examined here, is giving way to increasing formal control in the urbanized and heterogeneous societies in which they are located.

At the beginning of this study I posed the question on the exercise of power - by whom, over whom and by what means? It can now be seen that the answer that follows must be that power is exercised by neither state nor individual but an association of both. This is so even though the state retains the sovereign right to promote its policies of freedom of choice - through violence if it so wishes. Private security patrol is, thus, a strategy dependent not only upon the creation of state policy but upon certain fractions of the public themselves searching for substitution after experiencing a loss of security in their lives. Their are no wholly passive receivers of state control. This does not mean, however, that it is a non-oppressive and equitable strategy. On the contrary, a degree of oppression and inequality is clear from the research findings here. But this is created by a number of factors, each having its source within the structure of modern capitalism. Individuals, accordingly, have the capacity to participate in the creation of their own oppression.

This theoretical construction does not limit the model of order to a merely structural or social explanation but incorporates both these factors. A central element of this framework is the recognition that human agents' practices of reasoning may constitute the control forms on which policing is founded. People (security guards) are merely watching people (clients and potential offenders). There is no repressive and overbearing surveillance which has state structure as its base. It is simple surveillance that is dominant here and not the complex and structure-bound explanation of some left-functionalists. I advocate, accordingly, theoretical pluralism as representing the findings of this study. I believe this approach is more successful in explaining some of the developments occurring in the criminal justice system today.

Both subjectively and objectively the concepts of self-help and choice have been identified as central aspects of this study. Institutions of the state - the Audit Commission, the Home Office, the Police, the Private Security Sector and its personnel - are strong influences in the process of change. Personal gratification, however, is also a powerful element in the analysis. The market, presented by the state as an arena of free choice, is an institution through which the gratification of fears and desires can be channelled. Choice, rather than constraint, is the dominating factor of control and the catalyst in an interrelationship between agency and structure where neither dominates the other.

An embarrassment of choice

It has been argued that modern consciousness entails a vast movement from fate to choice in human affairs (Berger, 1979, p. 3). If this is so then how is it that many economically disadvantaged individuals are not part of this movement? And in a more general sense, if, as Berger suggests, choice is so much a characteristic of modern society why is the routine life of so many people so similar and why do institutions impose structures which reduce choice - for instance, the nine to five day and economic constraints on the type of schooling and health care available? And this lack of choice is at the centre of the present study. For while promising a rationally operated, impartial and universal system of justice, private security patrol in neighbourhoods has an inherently competitive classicist style which excludes freedom from those who are non-competitive. There is, accordingly, an embarrassing contradiction between formal and substantive equality - classicism promises too much freedom of choice.

Traditional public police ground has now become the beats of private security officers and this means that we cannot expect policing ethics to be as high as they were hitherto. This is because private security has an inherently competitive style and the market, from where private security is supplied, has a tendency to be unethical. And those of us who are non-competitive are likely to loose out on current crime prevention policies, which at best are elitist in nature. Accordingly, private security's promise of choice for all is an unobtainable promise - in today's less than equal society it cannot deliver it in reality. Its promises of 'community', 'fear reduction' and 'crime prevention' turn out to be contradictions of its actual disposition. It is not, therefore, conducive to the requirements of quality and equity of justice which are so crucial and intrinsic to the association policing should have with a democratic, equal and free society.

Policy implications: correcting a divergent trend

The analysis in this study has identified a mismatch between the primary (reactive) function of the public police (Reiss, 1980, 1983, 1987) and the way that social control currently tends to be moving - towards a more administrative, regulatory and proactive form (Kamenka and Tay, 1975; Foucault, op. cit.; Melossi, op. cit.; Mathiesen, op. cit.; Jayewardene, 1985). The criminal justice system has become increasingly interested in policies of preventative justice. These policies, which impose only preventative measures, concentrate on the individual primarily as a potential offender, not as a whole human being. It is clear that the private security industry is aligned more to this trend in prevention than are the public police, whose resources are directed mainly to reaction and detection.

A great deal of ill-judged criticism has recently been levelled at the police as they strive to meet the extraordinary demands on their time. But irrespective of the causation, the evidence suggests that the responsibility for protecting property is shifting inexorably towards other organizations and individuals as the main weight of police pressure concentrates on serious crime, racial tensions and concerted hooliganism (Wright, 1981, p. 108). Increased demands for police action involve more servicing and less and less enforcement (Bayley, 1980, p. 47).

The threat to consensus policing

Accordingly, traditional aspects of public policing are under challenge partly because the philosophy of economy, effectiveness and efficiency is forcing public police, whether managers or otherwise, to look for the quantifiable elements of policing such as measuring the crime detection rate. The interpenetration of public and private policing agencies identified in this study is influenced profoundly by state policy, which emphasises the use of quantifiable rather than symbolic forms of policing. These quantifiable elements relate almost exclusively to recordable crime statistics and not preventative measures taken to reduce crime. It is primarily upon these quantifiable elements of policework being conducive with effectiveness and efficiency that police forces obtain their funding from central government. It is not surprising, therefore, that public police policy concentrates on this aspect of social control, for to provide evidence of the effectiveness of symbolic, preventative forms of policing is a much more difficult problem for them than revealing simple statistics on those crimes they have detected or which remain undetected. In contrast, the strategy of neighbourhood private security patrol delivers not only evidence of actual prevention for those it serves, it also provides the symbolic element of policing provision which is so important to the ontological aspect of security inherent in us all. And the public police, in missing this point, may have their legitimacy threatened, for unless they can correct this divergent trend, by moving closer to the public through answering their demands for ontological security, there will be a greater threat to the traditional testimony that public police have the consent of the commonalty.

Located within the descriptive umbrella of 'community policing' the 'service' function of prevention is, unfortunately, often described by police as the 'soft end' of policework. Neglecting and underestimating the importance of preventative patrol in their community role appears to affect police legitimacy with the public. The consequences of this under-emphasis upon the unquantifiable aspects of policework may, thus, increase ineffectiveness. The overall loss in interaction between the police and the public created by the move away from a 'service' role has obvious implications for 'consensus policing' (Sherman, op. cit.; Bennett, 1987).

The notion that better relations with the public will increase the flow of criminal intelligence (Alderson, 1982) is now a central part of Home Office and public police strategy. The flow of information between the police and the public is crucial because when it comes to detection it is the public who influence this the most (Greenwood, Chaiken and Petersilia, op. cit.; Bottomley and Coleman, 1981). But the notion of increased intelligence through better relations together with these research findings must be taken more seriously - for it is indeed the public who detect the most crime through the information they possess and pass onto the police. This finding should not surprise because the public are the victims of and witnesses to crime. They therefore possess the information to assist the police to detect, arrest and successfully prosecute offenders. Thus, moving away from the community by failing to deal with the more mundane forms of policework will not assist the main objective of public police - public tranquillity. All this must result in a decrease in order as contact with the public diminishes - working at the 'hard end' will become increasingly more difficult for the police if the 'soft end' is neglected or forgotten altogether:

In an age when the emphasis in policing is on bringing police and community closer, there is a human contradiction inherent in privatization also. If the nature of the police organization is changed too radically towards a coercion-centred model, then the organization is no longer a suitable one to participate in the consensual type of police/public relationship that is the cornerstone of the British Policing style. (Dance, 1989, p. 296).

Beat policing could become the province of private security unless the Home Office and police managers have more effective objectives regarding the security of local people. It is not only the communities who have enlisted the services of private security that are demanding action from the public agency. Many other communities are sending clear messages that they need increased security. This demand will only be met if the public police provide a greater uniformed presence on the streets directed at specific neighbourhood problems. This demand is currently not being seriously addressed by the state institutions responsible for security. They must not lose sight of the fact that it is they who have the responsibility for providing an effective level of security for the whole of society - not just a fortunate few. One of the paramount aims of a system of police should be the reduction of tension in communities. But if communities are merely afraid of victimization then they are indeed the victims of crime. Police have a responsibility to avoid degrading people and help them to retain their dignity. Thus the moral and ethical principles of police must put persons before property - public police have this moral responsibility (Alderson, 1979).

Equal provision promoted

While it is hardly an objective of private police, public police policy should promote the equal provision of security as a professional ethic. There is here, however, an unfortunate paradox involving double standards. For this ethical notion of equality clashes with the state's present policy of promoting individual protection. Nevertheless, it would increase the credibility of public police if they took more seriously the phenomenon of crime deflection and its identification in practical terms. Indeed, professionalism would be enhanced by local police research to try and identify the targets of deflected crime and thereafter take action to resolve the problem by re-allocating resources.

Regulating private police will also help to reverse the trend in the fragmentation of society identified in this study. It seems a simple matter to use some form of licensing which would make the private sector more answerable. However, this may well legitimize further the use of private patrols in residential areas and accelerate community dysfunction by creating a proliferation of separate, privately protected areas. And as the professionalization of the private patrols increases there will be corresponding wage increases which will have to be offset by higher charges to clients. The inequity of social control in that model would be a further and perpetuating cause in polarisation - effective protection would become increasingly more available to those who could afford to pay.

A destructive laissez-faire approach

In a system where paying for protection and assurance is the only certain way of solving your problems - like paying for good health - there will be more casualties amongst those who cannot pay, or do not on principle want to pay. The communities most affected by this deterioration in control will inevitably be the most deprived. The very notion that the police are becoming more reactive than proactive will be exacerbated by the fragmented society which private provision creates. The laissez-faire approach to public/private co-operation represents the status-quo in the United Kingdom at the present time. Private security continues to develop in isolation from public organizational regulation. Co-operation is generally limited as each sector pursues its own objectives - the private sector working for a larger share of the market while the public police attempt to allocate scarce resources to meet the growing demand created by serious crime. For the public police long range planning is not possible as they respond to public demands which they cannot meet. In the meantime the market fills the gaps which the public sector cannot fill. Thus market forces, rather than fair policy, govern the quality of service and consequently the quality of justice.

The impact on police authority that this laissez-faire approach brings with it is ultimately damaging. For as the public turns more and more to private sources to provide the protection they feel they need, public police may find their authority gradually eroding. The consequences of loss of authority could well further undermine public confidence in police and raise the risk of the kind of aggressive citizen reaction that we have seen from time to time both in the USA and the United Kingdom. Unless we really want the polarisation of the public and the police and increased polarisation of classes, I believe that equal prevention is an alternative that the public police are seriously obliged to consider as the traditional providers of public security. They must therefore look away from the laissez-faire approach to a more radical alternative.

A radical alternative: towards security as a public corporation

Some public services, e.g. health, housing, are too socially important for market forces to dominate their provision. Public security must be included in this category. Private security, biased as it is in favour of wealth and power and selective in its provision in these areas, should not be allowed to dominate the provision of security. Only addressing society's inequalities will go anywhere near reaching a solution to unequal protection - superficial systems of co-operation between public and private will not change anything much.

In this age of advanced capitalism there are, however, obvious limitations about the possibilities of equality and I do not underestimate these inherent problems. But limits and possibilities should inform each other and it is sometimes more realistic to consider only the desirability of what can be done in terms of future policy. In this respect there exists a need for policy in security provision to be universally accessible. Such an ambitious position would, however, require a degree of radical social and institutional change. But before introducing the model of my radical alternative, in order to further legitimize its implementation a short return to the theoretical, and perhaps idealistic, will be necessary.

Insurance and security for society

The combination of agency and structure, or 'structuration' as it has been called (Giddens, 1984), has been shown in the present study not to provide equal and fair security provision. Thus, the inequitable culture of self-help and choice necessitates a more cohesive solidarity wherein effective policing provision is within the choice-range of all in society. In this respect, and in accordance with the findings of this study, I have taken my cue from Foucault, (op. cit.) in foretelling the future of neighbourhood security. The forecast is that as well as creating discipline upon the anatomo-politics of the human body there will be a regulatory, welfare, life-preserving effect upon the bio-politics of the population as insurance and security, become increasingly important to individuals and states (Foucault, ibid., p. 139). Thereafter society will be imbued with a cohesion which forms a specific solidarity (Smart, op. cit., p. 80). From this arrangement emerges the 'social' or the 'policing' of society, which has 'public happiness' as one of its main objects (Pasquino, op. cit.). This form of policing fits well with the form identified in this study, for it has an 'administrative' rather than disciplinary nature and is to be understood:

> ....not as the set of material and moral conditions that characterize a form of consolidation. It would appear to be the set of means which allow social life to escape material pressures and politico-moral uncertainties; the entire range of methods which make the members of society relatively safe from the effects of economic fluctuations by providing a certain security. (Donzelot, op. cit., p. xxvi).

This conclusion is also congruent with the notion of 'life politics', (Giddens, 1991, Chapter 7) for life politics issues, such as those demonstrated in the present study, call for:

> ....a remoralising of social life and they demand a renewed sensitivity to questions that the institutions of modernity systematically dissolve. (Donzelot, ibid., p. 224).

In so doing they return to prominence the same moral and existential questions repressed by the dominant institutions of modernity (Donzelot, ibid., p. 223).

If the law itself can act as a barrier against the exercise of arbitrary state power it can also be used in the process of change towards a less arbitrary system. In my conception of a future neighbourhood security system, accordingly, the legislative process will need to be invoked to introduce the public happiness through security alluded to by Foucault, Giddens and Pasquino. A compulsory national system of property insurance and security would provide the patrol personnel and other devices needed to enhanced security 'for' society. Preventative architectural hardware - alarms, various other security devices and contents insurance would also be available through this method. I envisage that this objective would be achieved through a state-directed enterprise, having its base in a partially nationalised insurance and security system. This would ensure universally applicable security provision running parallel to the open market. In this process individuals would be required to forgo a small degree of their freedom to choose in the market. But this is hardly a restriction on their freedom - given the gains to be made overall. Access to the market would of course be available still to those who wished to further enhance their individual security.

The theory behind such a model is that it combines the commercial freedom of private enterprise with the restriction of that freedom by a degree of government control. Partial share purchase by the government of the insurance and security sectors would be a simple and yet subtle form of public control. This would allow into the policing system a 'reflexive form of life politics' (Giddens, 1991, Chapters 6-7). Government profits, accrued through share purchase, would be compulsorily ploughed back into the public system. This would allow those without incomes to be supplemented. However, there is always a price to pay. Local councils would be required to raise a fixed proportion of the assets of individual households, relative to a total of the average income and value of property. The largest proportion of the precept would purchase patrol personnel and preventative hardware for the home. A proportion of the levy would be used by the local authority to purchase the most competitive contents insurance available.

Regulation through a cooperative alliance

The public would benefit from the combined efforts of private security services and public police providing quality crime control strategies (Meadows, 1984, p.51). An important part of this model would be a more controlled co-ordination between the public and private security sectors and between the private sector and local authorities. My vision coincides to some extent with those who would have a two-tier force:

> If a government were to embark on a programme of contracting out police services to competitive tender, it would have to be carefully thought out and orchestrated. It might begin by looking at all those services which do not require a fully trained, highly qualified and costly police officer. Here we begin to discern two levels of policing service. First the para-police, and second the police, as in the health service, where paramedics take much strain from the doctor resources. It is to the para-police services that the privatisation by contract might apply. (Alderson, 1991).

But I do not see a hiving-off of the non-crime role of police entirely to the private sector. Such an apparent wrench away from public service should not occur. There is ample evidence to show that the formation of a second-tier force, such as those in Canada and the USA (Slater, 1982a, 1982c), can be more aligned to public police and avoid reducing professional standards too much. Security companies would tender for council contracts to provide services and successful tenderers would forward lists of their staff to the police for vetting purposes. After successful vetting individuals would be sworn-in as special constables. They would have the same powers and wear the same uniform as regular officers but be identifiable as preventative police. The comparative reduction of the professional ability of these private personnel would be reflected in lower remuneration to that of their more highly trained colleagues. This improves the prospects of increasing the numbers of patrol personnel rather than pricing themselves into scarcity. There would exist a danger, however, that a lower rate of pay may attract a low standard of applicant and those of dubious character. This would need to be monitored carefully by recruiters.

With the assistance of the public police, private security firms who successfully tender for local patrol services would be required to train their staff in good policing practices and law. Such training would be provided by the police training department at the partial expense of the private firm. Such an arrangement would have the added benefit of personal contact between police and private security at an early working level. Shared training and a certain amount of controlled professional involvement could replace any negative stereotyping between agencies. In this model public-private relationships would be restructured by government control of training standards, supervision and quality of service.

Insurance and contract requirements could provide the stimulus for agreed-upon standards of performance. Insurance firms would indemnify private security organizations against civil action. A minimum level of training and certification would be required before employees were insured. There would be a financial incentive for firms to keep premiums low through their good practice and this would help quality-control and reduce a firms vulnerability to law. In this more cooperative system, policy makers, police managers and the police on the ground, could enter into cooperative agreements for the benefit of all. Police would be more willing to delegate authority to the private sector knowing that delegation could be withdrawn if a firm's certification were lost.

Police policy makers must fully accept that in the 1990's the primary resources for crime control are not with the public police. There is, thus, a need for more co-operation between public and private security. If the Home Office fail to accept the challenge of making informed judgements amongst alternative strategies, such as the model suggested here, they will not be providing the quality of service they really want to achieve. And if the analysis of this study is correct, they will also have missed an important moral opportunity to control the way that preventative policing will undoubtedly dominate the future of crime control.

But in relation to having any serious impact upon crime levels there is a sense in which these conclusions are too simplistic and unrealistic. It would be naive to imagine that if the model suggested here was in fact solely put into practice it would have any great impact upon crime levels. It must not be forgotten that such a model could only be substantially effective in association with other strategies. In view of this, not only must policy makers accept that the main resources for controlling crime do not lie with the public police, they must also accept that crime is the product not only of inadequate protection but that its causes too are pluralistic. They do include the situational and environmental causes discussed in this study, but they also include those more problematic and harder to resolve matters based in economic, social and political opportunity - matters to be influenced not by police, but by politicians. And these matters can only be affected through the state's serious commitment to providing a remoralization of social life by addressing the needs of ontological security for everyone.

Bibliography

Abel, R.L. (1982), *The Politics of Informal Justice*, Academic Press, New York.

Abrams, P. (1977), 'Community Care: Some Research Problems and Priorities' in Barnes, J. (ed.), Social Care Research, Bedford Square Press, Cambridge.

Adam Smith Institute (1989), *Wiser Councils: The Reform of Local Government*, Adam Smith Institute, London.

Adam Smith Institute (1991), *An Arresting Idea. The Management of Police Services in Modern Britain*, Adam Smith Institute, London.

Adelman, C. Jenkins, D. and Kemis, S. (1983), *Rethinking Case Study: Notes from the Second Cambridge Conference*, Deakin University, Victoria, Australia.

Aitkin, M. and Hage, J. (1964), 'The Organic Organization and Innovation', *Sociology*, Vol. 5.

Albanese, J.S. (1986), 'The Future of Policing: A Private Concern?', *Police Studies*, Summer.

Alderson, J. (1979), *Policing Freedom. A Commentary on the Dilemma of Policing in Western Democracies*, McDonald and Evans, Plymouth.

Alderson, J. (1982), 'The Case for Community Policing', in Cowell, D., Jones, T. and Young, J. (eds.), Policing the Riots, Junction Books, London.

Alderson, J. (1991), 'Policing by PLC', *Police*, May.

Aldrick, H. (1976), 'Resource Dependency and Interorganizational Relations Between Local Employment Service Sector Organizations', *Administration and Society*, Vol. 7.

Allatt, P. (1984a), 'Residential Security: Containment and Displacement of Burglary', *The Howard Journal of Criminal Justice*, Vol. 23, No. 2.

Allatt, P. (1984b), 'Fear of Crime: The Effect of Improved Residential Security on a Difficult to Let Estate', The Howard Journal of Criminal Justice, Vol. 23, No. 3.

Althusser, R.L. (1971), *Lenin and Philosophy and Other Essays*, New Left Bookshop, London.

Anderton, J. (1982), 'Crime and Security', Speech given at the opening of the New Central Police Station at Blackfriars House, Manchester, 8.3.1982., P and S Papers.

Arrow, K.J. (1951), *Social Choice and Individual Values*, Wiley, New York.

Arrow, K.J. (1973), 'Social Responsibility and Economic Efficiency', *Public Policy*, Vol. 21.

Ascher, K. (1987), *The Politics of Privatisation: Contracting Out Public Services*, MacMillan, London.

Audit Commission, (1983), *Improving Economy, Effectiveness and Efficiency in Local Government in England and Wales*, HMSO, London.

Audit Commission, (1984), *Report on Management of Local Authority Housing*, HMSO, London.

Bahan, C. (1974), 'The Reassurance Factor in Police Patrol', *Criminology*, Vol. 12.

Bailey, S. and Lynn, G. (1989), *The Private Security Industry - Towards 1992*, Northumbria Police Publications, Ponteland.

Baker, F. and O'Brien, G. (1971), 'Intersystems Relations and Coordination of Human Service Organization', *American Journal of Public Health*, Vol. 61, pp. 130-137.

Baker, M.H., Nienstedt, B.C., Everett, R.S. and McClery, R. (1983), 'The Impact of Crime Waves: Perception, Fear and Confidence in the Police', *Law and Society Review*, Vol. 17, pp. 319-335.

Balkin, S. and Houlden, P. (1983), 'Reducing Fear of Crime Through Occupational Presence', *Criminal Justice and Behaviour*, Vol. 10, pp. 13-33.

Baumer, T.L. (1978), 'Testing a General Model of Fear of Crime: Data From a National Sample', *Journal of Research in Crime and Delinquency*, Vols. 22 and 23, pp. 239-255.

Bayley, D.H. (1980), 'Ironies of American Law Enforcement', *The Public Interest*, Vol. 55, pp. 45-56.

Bayley, D.H. (1986), *Patterns of Policing. A Comparative International Analysis*, Rutgers University Press, New York.

Bayley, D.H. and Mendelsohn, H. (1969), *Minorities And The Police*, Free Press, New York.

Becker, H.S. (1968), 'Social Observation and Social Case Studies', *International Encyclopedia of the Social Sciences*, Vol. 11. Crowell, New York.

Becker, H.S. (1978), 'Problems Of Inference And Proof In Participant Observation', in Bynner, J. and Stribley, K.M. (eds.), *Social Research: Principles and Procedures*. pp. 312-324, Longman, New York.

Becker, T.M. (1973), 'The Place of Private Police in Society: An Area of Research for The Social Sciences', *Social Problems*, Vol. 21, No. 3, pp. 438-453.

Becton Council (1987), *Report of the Chief Housing Officer*, Document Dated 11th. March, Ref. CH087042, Bromley Council, Bromley, Kent.

Becton Council (1989), *Bromley's Management Style*, Special Projects Group, Bromley Council, Bromley, Kent.

Becton Council (1991), *Housing Investment Programme*, Strategy Statement, 1991/1992, Bromley Council, Bromley, Kent.

Belson, W.A. (1975), *Juvenile Theft: The Causal Factors*, Harper and Row, London.

Bennett, T.H. (1987), *An Evaluation of Two Neighbourhood Watch Schemes in London*, Cambridge Institute of Criminology, Cambridge.

Bensman, J. and Lilienfeld, R. (1979), *Between Public and Private: Lost Boundaries of the Self*, Free Press, London.

Benson, J.K. (1975), 'The Interorganizational Network of a Political Economy', *Administrative Science Quarterly*, Vol. 20, pp. 229-249.

Berger, P.L. and Luckman, T. (1967), *The Social Construction of Reality*, Allen Lane, London.

Berger, P.L., Berger, B and Kellner, H. (1974), *The Homeless Mind. Modernization and Consciousness*, Penguin, Harmondsworth.

Berger, P.L. (1979), *The Heretical Imperative. Contemporary Possibilities of Religious Affirmation*, Collins, London.

Berman, M. (1982), *All That Is Solid Melts Into Air*, Simon and Schuster, New York.

Bittner, E. (1970), *The Functions of The Police in Modern Society*, US Government Printing Office, Washington DC.

Bittner, E. (1974), 'A Theory of Police', in Jacob, H. (ed.), *The Potential For Reform Of Criminal Justice*, Sage, London.

Black, D.J. (1970), 'Production of Crime Rates', *American Sociological Review*, Vol. 35, pp. 733-748.

Black, D.J. (1971), 'The Social Organization of Arrest', *Stanford Law Review*, Vol. 23, pp. 1087-1111.

Boggs, S. (1971), 'Formal and Informal Crime Control: An Exploratory Study of Urban, Suburban and Rural Orientation', *Sociological Quarterly*, Vol. 12, pp. 319-327.

Boostrom, R.L. and Henderson, J.H. (1983), 'Community Action and, Crime Prevention: Some Unresolved Issues', *Crime and Social Justice*, Vol. 19, pp. 24-30.

Bottomley, K. and Coleman, C. (1980), 'Police Effectiveness and the Public: The Limitations of Official Crime Rates', in Clarke, R.V.G. and Hough, J.M. (eds.), *The Effectiveness of Policing*, pp. 70-97, Gower, Aldershot.

Bottomley, K. and Coleman, C. (1981), *Understanding Crime Rates*, Gower, Aldershot.

Bottoms, A.E. (1983), 'Neglected Features of Contemporary Penal Systems' in Garland, D. and Young, P. (eds.), *The Power to Punish: Contemporary Penality and Social Analysis*, pp. 166-202, Heinemann, London.

Brady, J.P. (1981), 'Sorting Out The Exile's Confusion: Or Dialogue On Popular Justice', *Contemporary Crises*, Vol. 5, pp. 155-192.

Brewer, J., Guelke, A., Hume, I., Moxon-Browne, E. and Wilford, R. (1988), *The Police, Public Order and the State*, MacMillan, London.

Brown, D. and Iles, S. (1985), 'Community Constables: A Study of a Police Initiative', in Heal, K., Tarling, R. and Burrows, J. (eds.), *Policing Today*, pp. 43-59, Home Office Research and Planning Unit, London.

Buchanan, J.M. (1978), *The Economics of Politics*, I.E.A. Readings, London.

Buchanan, J.M. and Tullock, G. (1981), 'An American Perspective: From Markets Work To Public Choice', in Seldon, A. (ed.), *The Emerging Consensus?*, I.E.A., London.

Burgess, E.W. (1925), 'Can Neighbourhood Work Have a Scientific Basis?', in Park, R.E., Burgess, E.W. and McKenzie, R., (eds.), *The City*, Chicago University Press, Chicago.

Burrows, J. and Lewis, H. (1988), *Directing Patrol Work*, Home Office Research Study Number 99, HMSO, London.

Burrows, J. and Tarling, R. (1987), 'The Investigation of Crime in England and Wales', *British Journal of Criminology*, No. 27, pp. 229-251.

Cain, M. (1979), 'Trends in The Sociology of Police Work', Paper Presented at the 8th. International Congress of Criminology, Lisbon, 4th.- 9th. September, 1978 and published in the *International Journal of Sociology of Law*, Vol. 7, No. 2, pp. 1-19.

Cannell, C.F. and Fowler, F.J. (1964), 'A Note on Interviewer Effect in Self Enumeration Procedure', *American Sociological Review*, Vol. 29, p. 270.

Carlen, P. (1976), *Magistrates Justice*, London, Martin Robertson.

Carr-Hill, R.A. and Stern, N.H. (1979), *Crime, The Police and Criminal Statistics,* Academic Press, New York.

Center, L.J. and Smith, T.G. (1973), 'Crime Statistics - Can They Be Trusted?', *American Criminal Law Review,* Vol. 11, pp. 1045-1086.

Chaiken, M. and Chaiken, J. (1987), *Public Policing Privately Provided,* Report Prepared for U.S. Department of Justice, National Institute of Justice, Washington.

Clarke, R.V.G. (1980), 'Situational Crime Prevention: Theory and Practice', *British Journal of Criminology,* Vol. 20, No. 2, pp. 136-147.

Clarke, R.V.G. and Mayhew, W.P. (1980), *Designing Out Crime,* HMSO, London .

Clemente, F. and Kleinman, M.B. (1977), 'Fear of Crime in the United States' *Social Forces,* Vol. 56, pp. 519-531.

Cohen, P. (1979), 'Policing the Working Class City', in Fine, B., Kinsey, R., Lea, J., Picciotto, S. and Young, J. (eds.), *Capitalism and the Rule of Law: From Deviancy Theory to Marxism,* pp. 118-136, Hutchinson, London.

Cohen, S. (1979), 'The Punitive City: Notes On The Dispersal Of Social Control', *Contemporary Crisis: Crime, Law and Social Policy,* Vol. 3, pp. 339-363.

Cohen, S. (1981), 'Footprints in the Sand: A Further Report on Criminology and the Sociology of Deviance in Britain', in Fitzgerald, M., McLennan, G and Pawson, J. (eds.), *Crime and Society, Readings in History and Theory,* pp. 220-247, Routledge and Kegan Paul, London.

Cohen, S. (1985), *Visions of Social Control: Crime, Punishment and Classification,* Polity Press, Cambridge.

Cohen, S. and Scull, A. (1983), *Social Control and the State,* Martin Robertson, Oxford.

Comrie, M.D. and Kings, E.J. (1975), *Study of Urban Workloads,* Police Research Services, Report No. 11, Home Office, London.

Conklin, J.E. (1971), 'Dimensions of Community Response to the Crime Problem', *Social Problems,* Vol. 18, pp. 373-385.

Conklin, J.E. (1975), *The Impact of Crime,* Prentice Hall, New Jersey.

Cook, K. (1977), 'Exchange and Power in Networks of Organizational Relations', *Sociological Quarterly,* Vol. 18, pp. 62-82.

Cordner, G.W. (1986), 'Fear of Crime and the Police: An Evaluation of a Fear Reduction Strategy', *Journal of Police Science and Administration,* Vol.14, No. 3, pp. 223-233.

Cornish, D.B. and Clarke, R.V.G. (1986), 'Situational Prevention, Displacement of Crime and Rational Choice Theory', in Heal, K. and Laycock, G. (eds.), *Situational Crime Prevention: From Theory into Practice'*, Home Office, HMSO, London.

Cornish, D.B. and Clarke, R.V.G. (1988), 'Understanding Crime Displacement: An Application of Rational Choice Theory', *Criminology*, Vol. 7, pp. 933-947.

Critchley, T. (1978), *The History of the Police in England and Wales*, Constable, London.

Cumming, E. (1968), *Systems of Social Regulation*, Atherton Press, New York.

Cumming, E., Cumming, I. and Edell, L. (1965), 'Policeman as Philosopher, Guide and Friend', *Social Problems*, Vol. 12, pp. 276-286.

Currie, E. (1988), 'Two Visions of Community Crime Prevention', in Hope, T. and Shaw, M. (eds.), *Communities and Crime Reduction*, HMSO, London.

Dance, O.R. (1989), 'To What Extent Could or Should Policing be Privatized?', The 1989 Queen's Police Gold Medal Essay. *The Police Journal*, Vol. 33, No. 4, pp. 288-297.

Dean, J.P. and Whyte, W.F. (1978), 'How Do You Know If The Informant Is Telling The Truth?', in Bynner, J. and Stribley, K.M. (eds.), *Social Research: Principles and Procedure*, pp. 179-185, Longman, Essex.

de Sousa Santos, B. (1979), 'Popular Justice, Duel Power and Socialist Strategy', in Fine, B., Kinsey, R., Lea, J., Picciotto, S. and Young, J. (eds.), *Capitalism And The Rule Of Law: From Deviancy Theory To Marxism*, pp. 151-163, Hutchinson, London.

Denzin, N. (1970), *The Research Act*, Aldine, Chicago.

Donovan, E.J. and Walsh, W.F. (1986), *An Evaluation of Starrett City Security Services*, Pennsylvania State University.

Donzelot, J. (1979), *The Policing of Families*, Pantheon Books, New York.

Dunleavy, P. and O' Leary, B. (1987), *Theories Of The State: The Politics Of Liberal Democracy*, MacMillan, London.

Durkheim, E. (1897), *Suicide: A Study in Sociology*, Free Press, Glencoe.

East Sussex Police, (1919), *Code Of Rules And Regulations*, Police Headquarters, Sussex.

Edelman, M. (1964), *The Symbolic Uses of Politics*, University of Illinois Press, Urbana.

Elliott, N. (1989), *Streets Ahead*, The Adam Smith Institute, London.

Epstien, C. (1962), *Intergroup Relations with Police Officers*, Wilkins and Wilkins, Baltimore.

Erikson, K. (1966), *Wayward Puritans*, Wiley, New York.

Evan, W. M. (1962), 'Public and Private Legal Systems', in Evan, W.M. (ed.), *Law and Sociology, Exploratory Essays*, pp. 165-184, Greenwood, Westport, Connecticut.

Ewan, S. and Ewan, E. (1982), *Channels of Desire*, McGraw-Hill, New York.

Fielding, N.G. (1991), *The Police and Social Conflict: Rhetoric and Reality*, Athlone Press, London and Atlantic Highlands, NJ.

Foucault, M. (1979a), *Discipline and Punish: The Birth of The Prison*, Penguin, London.

Foucault, M. (1979b), *The History of Sexuality*, Volume 1, An Introduction, Allen Lane, London.

Fowler, F.J., McCalla, M.E. and Mangione, T.W. (1979), *Reducing Residential Crime and Fear: The Hartford Neighbourhood Crime Prevention Programme - Executive Summary*, National Institute of Law Enforcement and Criminal Justice, Washington DC.

Fox, R.W. and Lears, T.J.J. (1983), *The Culture of Consumption*, Pantheon Books, New York.

Fromm, E. (1941), *Escape from Freedom*, Holt, Rinehart and Wilson, London.

Friedman, M. (1962), *Capitalism and Freedom*, University of Chicago Press, Chicago.

Gabor, T. (1981), 'The Crime Displacement Hypothesis: An Empirical Examination', *Crime and Delinquency*, July, pp. 390-404.

Galbraith, A.J.K. (1969), *The Affluent Society*, Hamilton, New York.

Gallati, R. (1983), *Introduction to Private Security*, Eaglewood Cliffs, Prentice Hall, New Jersey.

Gallup. (1982), *Gallup Political Index No. 260, April, 1982*, Social Surveys (Gallup Poll), Ltd. London.

Gamble, A. (1981), *Britain in Decline*, MacMillan, London.

Garland, D. (1990), 'Frameworks of Enquiry in The Sociology of Punishment', *The British Journal of Sociology*, Vol. 41, No. 1, pp. 1-15.

Garland, D. and Young, P. (eds.), (1983), *The Power to Punish. Contemporary Penality and Social Analysis*, Heinemann, London.

Garofalo, J. (1981), 'The Fear of Crime and its Consequences', *Journal of Criminal Law and Criminology*, No. 72, pp. 829-857.

George, V. and Wilding, P. (1985), *Ideology and Social Welfare*, Routledge and Kegan Paul, London.

Giddens, A. (1973), *The Class Structure of Advanced Societies*, Hutchinson, London.

Giddens, A. (1979), *Central Problems in Social Theory, Action Structure And Contradictions In Social Analysis*, Macmillan, London.

Giddens, A. (1981), *A Contemporary Critique of Historical Materialism*, Vol. 1, MacMillan, London.

Giddens, A. (1984), *The Constitution of Society*, Polity Press, Cambridge.

Giddens, A. (1991), *Modernity and Self Identity. Self and Society in the Late Modern Age*, Polity Press, Cambridge.

Gilbert, N. and Gilbert, B. (1989), *The Enabling State. Modern Welfare Capitalism in America*, Oxford University Press, Oxford.

Gladstone, F.J. (1980), *Coordinating Crime Prevention Efforts*, Home Office Research Study No. 62, HMSO, London.

Glennerster, H., Power, A. and Travers, T. (1991), 'A New Era for Social Policy: A New Enlightenment or a New Leviathan?', *Journal of Social Policy*, Vol. 20, No. 3, pp. 389-414.

Goetz, J.P. and Lecompte, M.D. (1984), *Ethnography and Qualitative Design in Educational Research*, Academic Press, Orlando, Florida.

Gramsci, A. (1971), *Selections from the Prison Notebooks*, Lawrence and Wishard, London.

Greenberg, S.W., Rohe, W.M. and Williams, J.R. (1982), *Safe and Secure Neighbourhoods: Physical Characteristics and Informal Territorial Control in High and Low Crime Neighbourhoods*, US Department of Justice and National Institute of Justice, Washington DC.

Greenberg, S.W., Rohe, W.M. and Williams, J.R. (1985), *Informal Citizen Action and Crime Prevention at Neighbourhood Level*, Government Printing Office, Washington D.C.

Greenwood, P.W., Chaiken, J.M. and Petersilia, J. (1977), *The Criminal Investigation Process*, Heath, Massachusetts DC.

Guba, E.G. and Lincoln, Y.S. (1981), *Effective Evaluation*, Jossey-Bass, San Francisco.

Guest, D. (1984), 'Social Policy in Canada', *Social Policy and Administration*, Vol. 18, No. 2, pp. 30-147.

Gusfield, J.R. (1975), *Community: A Critical Response*, Basil Blackwell, Oxford.

Hackler, J.C., Ho, K.Y. and Urquhart-Ross, C. (1974), 'The Willingness to Intervene: Differing Community Characteristics', *Social Problems*, Vol.21, pp. 328-344.

Hall, R., Clark, J., Giordano, P., Johnson, P. and Van Roekel, M. (1977), 'Patterns of Inter-Organizational Relationships', *Administrative Science Quarterly*, Vol. 22, pp. 457-474.

Hall, S., Critcher, C., Jefferson, T., Clarke, J. and Roberts, B. (1978), *Policing the Crisis: Mugging, the State, Law and Order*, MacMillan, London.

144

Hall, S. and Scraton, P. (1981), 'Law, Class and Control', in Fitzgerald, M., McLennan, G. and Pawson, J. (eds.), *Crime and Society: Readings in History and Theory*, pp. 460-497, Kegan Paul, London.

Hayek, F.A. (1949), *Individualism and Economic Order*, Routledge and Kegan Paul, London.

Hayek, F.A. (1976), *Law, Legislation and Liberty, Vol.2, The Mirage of Social Justice*, Routledge and Kegan Paul, London.

Heal, K. and Laycock, G. (1986), *Situational Crime Prevention: From Theory into Practice*, HMSO, London.

Henderson, J.H. (1987), 'Public Law Enforcement, Private Security and Citizen Crime Prevention: Competition or Co-operation', *Police Journal*, January, pp. 48-57.

Hilliard, B. (1989), 'Into the 1990's', *Police Review*, 6th. October, pp. 2028-2029.

Hirsch, F. (1977), *Social Limits to Growth*, Routledge and Kegan Paul, London.

Hirschman, A.O. (1970), *Exit, Voice and Loyalty*, Harvard University Press, Cambridge, MA.

Holloway, J. and Picciotto, S. (1977), 'Capitalism, Crisis and the State', *Capitalism and Class*, No. 2, pp. 77-101.

Home Office. (1979), *The Private Security Industry: A Discussion Paper*, HMSO, London.

Home Office. (1983), *Manpower, Effectiveness and Efficiency in the Police Service*, Circular 114/1983.

Home Office. (1984), *Crime Prevention*, Circular 8/1984.

Home Office. (1989), *Practical Ways To Crack Crime*, HMSO, London.

Hope, T. (1988), 'Support for Neighbourhood Watch. A British Crime Survey Analysis', in Hope, T. and Shaw, W. (eds.), *Communities and Crime Reduction*, pp. 146-161, HMSO, London.

Hope, T. and Shaw, M. (eds.), (1988), *Communities and Crime Reduction*, HMSO, London.

Hough, M. (1989), 'Demand For Policing and Police Performance: Progress and Pitfalls in Public Surveys', in Weatheritt, M. (ed.) *Police Research: Some Future Prospects*, pp. 45-51, Avebury, Aldershot.

Hough, M. and Mayhew, P. (1983), *The British Crime Survey*, Home Office Research Study No. 76, HMSO, London.

Hunter, A. (1974), *Symbolic Communities*, University of Chicago Press, Chicago.

Huxley, A. (1932), *Brave New World: A Novel*, Chatto and Windus, London.

Ignatieff, M. (1978), *A Just Measure of Pain*, MacMillan, London.

Ignatieff, M. (1983), 'State, Civil Society and Total Institutions: A Critique of Recent Social Histories of Punishment', in Cohen, S. and Scull, A.T. (eds.), *Social Control and The State*, Basil Blackwell, London.

Jacobs, J. (1961), *The Death and Life of Great American Cities*, Random House, New York.

Jayewardene, C.H.S. (1985), 'Policing in the Future', *Crimecare Journal*, Vols. 1 and 2, pp. 138-155.

Jefferson, T. (1990), *The Case Against Paramilitary Policing*, Open University Press, Milton Keynes.

Jeffery, C.R. (1971), *Crime Prevention Through Environmental Design*, Sage, Beverly Hills.

Johnson, T.J. (1972), *Professions and Power*, MacMillan, London.

Johnson, T.J. (1976), 'Work and Power', in Esland, G. and Salaman, G. (eds.), *Politics of Work and Occupations*, Open University Press, Milton Keynes.

Jupp, V. (1989), *Methods of Criminological Research*, Unwin Hyman, London.

Kafka, F. (1930), *The Castle*, Martin, Secker and Warburg, London.

Kakalik, J.S. and Wildhorn, S. (1972), *Private Police in the United States: Findings and Recommendations*, Government Printing Office, Washington.

Kamenka, E. and Tay, A.E. (1975), 'Beyond Bourgeois Individualism: The Contemporary Crisis in Law and Legal Ideology', in Kamenka, E. and Neale, R.S. (eds.) *Feudalism, Capitalism and Beyond*, Edward Arnold, London.

Kasarda, J.D. and Janowitz, M. (1974), 'Community Attachment in Mass Society', *American Sociological Review*, Vol. 39, pp. 328-339.

Katzman, M.T. (1980), 'The Contribution of Crime to Urban Decline', *Urban Studies*, Vol. 17, pp. 277-286.

Keeton, G. (1975), *Keeping the Peace*, Barry Rose, London.

Keller, S.I. (1968), *The Urban Neighbourhood*, Random House, New York.

Keller, R. (1978), 'Boundary Spanning Activity, Role Dynamics and Job Satisfaction: A Longitudinal Study', *Journal of Business Research*, Vol. 61, pp. 147-158.

Kelling, G., Pate, T., Dieckman, D. and Brown, C. (1974), *The Kansas City Preventative Patrol Experiment: A Summary Report*, Police Foundation, Washington D.C.

Kerner, H.J. (1978), 'Fear of Crime and Attitudes Towards Crime: Comparative Criminological Reflections', *International Annals of Criminology*, Vol. 17, pp. 83-102.

Kinsey, R., Lea, J. and Young, J. (1986), *Losing The Fight Against Crime*, Basil Blackwell, London.

Klein, L. and Luxenburg, J. (1987), *Little Daughter Is Watching You: A Legalistic and Moral Assessment of Citizen Crime Reporting Activity*, Paper presented at The Academy of Criminal Justice Sciences, St.Louis, MO.

Klein, L., Luxenburg, J. and King, M. (1989), 'Perceived Neighbourhood Crime and the Impact of Private Security', *Crime and Delinquency*, Vol. 3, pp. 365-377.

Kohfeld, C.W. and Sprague, J. (1990), 'Demography, Police Behaviour and Deterrence', *Criminology*, Vol. 28, No. 1, pp. 111-136.

Lambert, J.R. (1970), Crime, Police and Race Relations, Oxford University Press, London.

Latessa, E.J. and Allen, H.E. (1980), 'Using Citizens To Prevent Crime; An Example Of Deterrence and Community Involvement', *Journal Of Police Science and Administration'*, Vol. 8, pp. 69-74.

Latessa, E.J. and Travis, L.F. (1986), *Criminal Opportunity Reduction Effort: Problems and Perspectives in Citizen Crime Prevention*, Paper presented at the Academy of Criminal Justice Sciences, Orlando, Florida.

Lavrakas, P.J., Normoyle, J., Skogan, J., Herz, E.J., Salem, C. and Lewis, D.A. (1980), *Factors Related To Citizen Involvement in Personal, Household and Neighbourhood Anti Crime Measures*, Final Report for National Institute of Justice, Northwestern University, Centre for Urban Affairs and Policy Research, Evanston, Illinois.

Lavrakas, P.J. and Herz, E.J. (1982), Citizen Participation in Neighbourhood Crime Prevention, *Criminology*, Vol. 20, pp. 479-498.

Lavrakas, P.J. and Bennett, T. (1985), *The Bubble-Up Approach To Community Anti-Crime Programming*, Paper presented at the Annual Meeting of the American Psychological Association, Los Angeles.

Lee, D and Newby, H. (1983), *The Problem of Sociology*, Hutchinson, London.

Leifer, R. and Delbecq, A. (1978), 'Organizational/Environmental Interchange: A Model of Boundary Spanning Activity', *Academy of Management Review*, Vol. 3, pp. 40-48.

Lenski, G.E. and Leggett, J.C. (1960), 'Caste, Class and Deference in the Research Interview', *The American Journal of Sociology*, Vol. 65, pp. 463-467.

Levine, S. and White, P.E. (1961), Exchange as a Conceptual Framework for the Study of Interorganizational Relationships, *Administrative Science Quarterly*, Vol. 5, pp. 583-601.

Liege, M.P. (1988), 'The Fight Against Crime and Fear: A New Initiative in France', in Hope, T. and Shaw, M. (eds.) *Communities and Crime Reduction*, pp. 254-259, HMSO, London.

Likert, R. (1932), 'A Technique for the Measurement of Attitudes', *Archives of Psychology*, No. 40.

Litwak, E. and Hylton, L. (1962), 'Interorganizational Analysis: A Hypothesis on Coordinating Agencies', *Administrative Science Quarterly*, Vol. 6, pp. 395-420.

Lowman, J., Menzies, R.J. and Palys, T.S. (eds.) (1987), *Transcarceration: Essays In The Sociology of Social Control*, Gower, Aldershot.

Lustgarten, L. (1986), *The Governance of Police*, Sweet and Maxwell, London.

MacBarnet, D.J. (1982), *Conviction: Law, The State and the Construction of Justice*, MacMillan, London.

MacCoby, E. and MacCoby, N. (1954), 'The Interview: A Tool of Social Science', in Gardner, L. (ed.) *Handbook of Social Psychology*, Vol. 1, Addison-Wesley, Cambridge, Mass.

Maguire, M. and Bennett, T. (1982), *Burglary in a Dwelling: The Offence, The Offender and The Victim*, Heinemann, London.

Maitland, F. (1913), *Constitutional History*, Cambridge University Press, Cambridge.

Manning, P.K. (1977), *Police Work: The Social Organization of Policing*, MIT Press, London.

Marplan. (1983), Survey carried out for BBC, Broadcasting Research Department, 22-24 August.

Marx, G.T. (1987), 'The Interweaving of Public and Private Police in Undercover Work', in Shearing, C.D. and Stenning, P.C. (eds.), *Private Policing*, pp. 172-193, Sage, London.

Marx, G.T. (1989), 'Commentary: Some Trends and Issues in Citizen Involvement in the Law Enforcement Process', *Crime and Delinquency*, Vol. 3, pp. 500-519.

Marx, G.T. and Archer, D. (1971), 'Citizen Involvement in the Law Enforcement Process: The Case of Community Police Patrols', *American Behavioural Scientist*, Vol. 15, p. 57.

Mathiesen, T. (1974), *The Politics of Abolition*, Martin Robinson, London.

Mathiesen, T. (1983), 'The Future of Control Systems - The Case of Norway', in Garland, D. and Young, P. (eds.), *'The Power to Punish: Contemporary Penality and Social Analysis*, pp. 130-145, Heinemann, London.

Mathiesen, T. (1987), 'The Eagle and the Sun: On Panoptical Systems and Mass Media in Modern Society', in Lowman, J., Menzies, R.J. and Palys, T.S., (eds.), *Transcarceration: Essays in the Sociology of Social Control*, pp. 59-75, Gower, Aldershot.

Mawby, R.I. (1979), *Policing the City*, Saxon House, Farnborough.

Maxfield, M. (1984), *Fear of Crime in England and Wales*, Home Office Research Study No. 78, HMSO, London.

Mayhew, P.M., Clarke, R.V.G., Sturman, A. and Hough, J.M. (1976), *Crime as Opportunity*, Home Office Research Study No. 34, HMSO, London.

Meadows, R. (1984), 'Private Security and Public Safety: Developments and Issues', *Journal Of Security Administration*, Vol. 7, No. 2, pp. 51-61.

Melossi, D. (1979), 'Institutions of Social Control and Capitalist Organization of Work', in Fine, B., Kinsey, R., Lea, J., Picciotto, S. and Young, J. (eds.), *Capitalism and the Rule of Law: From Deviancy Theory to Marxism*, pp. 90-99, Hutchinson, London.

Melossi, D. and Pavarani, M. (1981), *The Prison and The Factory: Origins of the Penitentiary System*, MacMillan, London.

Merry, S.E. (1981), *Urban Danger. Life in a Neighbourhood of Strangers*, Temple University Press, Philadelphia.

Metropolitan Police. (1836), *Police Instructions/Orders*, HMSO, London.

Minar, W. and Greer, S. (1969), *The Concept of Community: Readings with Interpretations*, Aldine, Chicago.

Minford, P. (1987), 'The Role of the Social Services: A View from the New Right', in Loney, M., Bowcock, R., Clarke, J., Cochrane, A., Graham, P. and Wilson, M., (eds.), *The State or the Market. Politics and Welfare in Contemporary Britain*, pp. 70-82, Sage, London.

Misner, G. (1967), 'The Urban Police Mission', *Issues in Criminology*, Vol. 3, pp. 35-46.

Moore, C. and Brown, J. (1981), *Community Versus Crime*, National Council for Community Organizations, Bedford Square Press, London.

Mosca, G. (1939), *The Ruling Class*, McGraw-Hill, London.

Newcastle Journal, (1988), *Private Security Officers Have Been Hired to Patrol a North Housing Estate After Reports of Rising Burglary and Vandalism*, October, 12th.

Newman, K. (1985), *A Selection of Speeches by Sir Kenneth Newman, QPM, Commissioner of Police of Metropolis*, Opening of the IFSSEC Exhibition, April, 15th., New Scotland Yard, London.

Newman, O. (1972), *Defensible Space: Crime Prevention Through Urban Design*, MacMillan, New York.

Newton, A. (1978), 'Prevention of Crime and Delinquency', *Criminal Justice Abstracts*, Vol, 10, No. 2, pp. 245-266.

Normandeau, A. (1968), *Trends and Patterns in the Crime of Robbery*, University Microfilms, Ann Arbor.

Nowell-Smith, G. (1980), 'In a State', *Screen Education*, pp. 5-10.

O'Connor, J. (1973), *The Fiscal Crisis of the State*, St. Martin's, New York.

O'Higgins, M. (1987), *Privatization and Social Welfare: Concepts Analysis and the British Experience*, University Press, Princeton.

O'Malley, P. (1988), 'Marxist Theory and Marxist Criminology', *Crime and Social Justice*, Vol. 29, pp. 70-87.

Olson, M. (1965), *The Logic of Collective Action*, Harvard University Press, Cambridge Massachusetts.

Oppenheim, A.N. (1979), 'The Quantification of Questionnaire Data', in Bynner, J. and Stribley, K.M. (eds.) *Social Research: Principles and Procedures*, pp. 208-224, Longman, Essex.

Packard, N. (1967), *The Hidden Persuaders*, Penguin, Harmondsworth.

Pancake, D. (1983), 'The New Professionals: Co-operation Between Police Departments and Private Security', *The Police Chief*, June, pp. 34-36.

Pareto, V. (1966), *Sociological Writings*, Pall Mall Press, London.

Parks, E. (1970)' 'From Constabulary to Police Society: Implications for Social Control', *Catalyst*, Vol. 5, pp. 76-97.

Pascal, A.H. and Menchik, M.D. (1979), *Fiscal Containment: Who Gains? Who Loses?* The Rand Corporation, Santa Monica, Califonia.

Pasquino, P. (1978), 'Theatrum Politicum. The Genealogy of Capital - Police and the State of Prosperity', *Ideology and Consciousness*, Vol. 4, pp. 41-54.

Pate, A.M. and Wycoff, M.A. (1986), *Reducing Fear of Crime in Houston Newark*, Police Foundation, Washington DC.

Pearson, G. (1983), *Hooligan: A History of Respectable Fears*, MacMillan, London.

Pease, K. and Barr, R. (1990), 'Crime Placement, Displacement and Deflection: A Review of Research', in Tonry, M. and Norris, N. (eds.), *Crime and Justice*, Vol. 12, pp. 277-318, University of Chicago Press, Chicago.

Perkin, H. (1969), *Theories of Modern English Society*, Routledge, London.

Picciotto, S. (1979), 'The Theory of The State, Class Struggle And The Rule Of Law', in Fine, B., Kinsey, R., Lea, J., Picciotto, S. and Young, J. (eds.) *Capitalism And The Rule Of Law: From Deviancy Theory To Marxism*, pp. 164-177, Hutchinson, London.

Pitkin, H. (1981), 'Justice: On Relating Private and Public', *Political Theory*, Vol. 9, No. 3, pp. 327-352.

Plant, R. (1978), 'Community: Concept, Conception, and Ideology', *Politics and Society*, Vol. 8, No. 1, p. 81.

Platt, T. and Takagi, P. (1981), 'Intellectuals for Law and Order: A Critique of the New Realists', in Platt, T. and Takagi, P., (eds.), *Crime and Social Justice*, MacMillan, London.

Operational Policing Review, (1990), The Joint Consultative Committee, Surrey.

Police Review, (1989a), 'Nibbling Away At The Bobbies Patch', January, 13th. pp. 64-65.

Police Review, (1989b), 'Private Security Doubled in Four Years', July, 14th., p. 1406.

Police Review, (1989c), Tenants Pay 40p a Week For Security Patrols, April, 14th. pp. 740-741.

Poulantzas, N. (1973), *Political Power And Social Class*, New Left Books, London.

Power, N. (1987), *Property Before People*, Allen and Unwin, London.

Punch, M. and Naylor, T. (1973), 'The Police: A Social Service', *New Society*, Vol. 24, pp. 358-361.

R. v Howell (1981), *Criminal Law Review*, No. 524.

R. v Podger (1979), *Criminal Law Review*, No. 524.

Radzinowicz, L. (1956), *A History of English Criminal Law and its Administration from 1750*, Vols. 2 and 3, Stevens, London.

Randall, W. and Hamilton, P. (1972), 'The Security Industry of the United Kingdom' in Hamilton, P., Wiles, P. and McClintock, F. (eds.), *The Security Industry in the United Kingdom*, Institute of Criminology, University of Cambridge, Cambridge.

Readers' Digest, (1987), 'Armchair Detectives Get Their Man', May, pp. 109-114.

Reichman, N. (1987), 'The Widening Webs of Surveillance: Private Police Unravelling Deceptive Claims', in Shearing, D. and Stenning, P.C. (eds.), *Private Policing*, pp. 247-265, Sage, London.

Reid, W. (1964), 'Interagency Coordination in Delinquency Prevention and Control', in Stratton, J.R. and Terry, R.M. (eds.), *Prevention of Delinquency*, MacMillan, London.

Reiss, A.J. (1980), *Policing in the Year 2,000*, Law Enforcement and Society Symposium, Ottawa.

Reiss, A.J. (1983), 'The Policing of Organizational Life', in Punch, M. (ed.), *Control in the Police Organization*, MIT, London.

Reiss, A.J. (1987), 'The Legitimacy of Intrusion Into Private Space', in Shearing, C.D. and Stenning, P.C. (eds.), *Private Policing*, Sage, London.

Reppetto, T.A. (1974), *Residential Crime*, Ballinger, Cambridge, M.A.

Reppetto, T.A. (1976), 'Crime Prevention and the Displacement Phenomenon', *Crime and Delinquency*, pp. 166-177.

Ridley, N. (1988), *The Local Right: Enabling Not Providing*, Centre for Policy Studies, London.

Rosenbaum, D.P. (1988), 'A Critical Eye on Neighbourhood Watch: Does It Reduce Crime and Fear?', in Hope, T. and Shaw, M. (eds.), *Communities and Crime Reduction*, pp. 126-145, HMSO, London.

Roshier, R. (1989), *Controlling Crime: The Classical Perspective in Criminology*, Open University Press, Milton Keynes.

Rowe, C. (1986), *People and Chips: The Human Implications of Information Technology*, Paradigm, London.

Rusche, G. and Kircheimer, O. (1939), *Punishment and Social Structure*, Columbia University Press, New York.

Rutter, M. and Giller, H. (1983), *Juvenile Delinquency: Trends and Perspectives*, Penguin, Harmondsworth.

Saks, M. (1983), 'Removing the Blinkers: A Critique of Recent Contributions to the Sociology of the Professions', *Sociological Review*, Vol. 31, pp. 1-21.

Savas, E.S. (1983), *Privatising The Public Sector. How to Shrink Government*, Chatham House, New Jersey.

Schmidt, S.M. and Kochan, T. (1972), 'The Concept of Conflict', *Administrative Science Quarterly*, Vol. 17, pp. 359-370.

Schmidt, S.M. and Kochan, T. (1977), 'Interorganizational Relationships, Patterns, Motivations', *Administrative Science Quarterly*, Vol. 22, pp. 220-234.

Schnelle, J.F., Kirchner, R.E., McNees, M.P. and Lawler, J.M. (1975), 'Social Evaluation Research: The Evaluation of Two Police Patrolling Strategies', *Journal of Applied Behaviour Analysis*, Vol. 8, pp. 353-365.

Schutz, A. (1962), *Collected Papers*, Vol. 1., Martinus Nijhoff, The Hague.

Seidman, D. and Couzens, M. (1974), 'Getting the Crime Rate Down: Political Pressure and Crime Reporting', *Law and Society Review*, Vol. 8, pp. 457-493.

Seligman, B.B. (1973), 'Max Weber And The Capitalist Spirit', in Recktenwald, H.C., (ed.), *Political Economy: An Historical Perspective*, pp. 348-356, Collier MacMillan, London.

Sellin, T. and Wolfgang, M. (1964), *The Measurement of Delinquency*, Wiley, New York.

Shapland, J. and Vagg, J. (1988), *Policing By The Public*, Routledge, London.

Shearing, C.D., Farnell, M. and Stenning, P.C. (1980), *Contract Security in Ontario*, University of Toronto, Toronto Centre of Criminology.

Shearing, C.D. and Stenning, P.C. (1981), 'Modern Private Security: Its Growth and Implications', in Tonry, M. and Morris, N. (eds.), *Crime and Justice: An Annual Review of Research,* Vol. 3, pp. 193-245, University of Chicago Press, Chicago.

Shearing, C.D and Stenning, P.C. (1982), 'Snowflakes or Good Pinches? Private Security's Contribution to Modern Policing', in Donelan, R. (ed.) *The Maintenance of Order in Society,* pp. 96-105, Canadian Police College, Ottawa.

Shearing, C.D. and Stenning, P.C. (1983), 'Private Security: Implications for Social Control', *Social Problems,* Vol. 30, No. 5, pp. 492-506.

Shearing, C.D. and Stenning, P.C. (eds.) (1987a), *Private Policing,* Sage, London.

Shearing, C.D. and Stenning, P.C. (1987b), 'Say Cheese!: The Disney Order That Is Not So Mickey Mouse', in Shearing, C.D. and Stenning, P.C. (eds.), *Private Policing,* pp. 317-323, Sage, London.

Sherman, L.W. (1983), 'Patrol Strategies for Police', in Wilson, J.Q. (ed.) *Crime and Public Policy,* pp. 145-163, ICS Press, San Francisco.

Siatt, W. (1981), 'Contract/Proprietary Guards: How they Suit User's Needs', *Security World,* July, pp. 21-35.

Skogan, W.G. (1987), *Disorder and Community Decline,* Final Report to the National Institute of Justice, Northwestern University, Evanston, Ill.

Skogan, W.G. (1988), 'Community Organizations and Crime', in Tonry, M. and Morris, N., (eds.) *Crime and Justice,* Vol. 10, pp. 39-78.

Skogan, W.G. (1990), *The Police and Public in England and Wales: A British Crime Survey Report,* HMSO, London.

Skogan, W.G. and Maxfield, M.G. (1981), *Coping With Crime: Individual and Neighbourhood Reactions,* Sage, Beverly Hills.

Skolnick, J.H. (1966), *Justice Without Trial,* Wiley, London.

Skolnick, J.H. and Bayley, D.H. (1986), *The New Blue Line: Police Innovation in Six American Cities,* Collier MacMillan, London.

Slater, T. (1982a), 'Police and Security', *Police Review,* 8th. January, pp. 19-22.

Slater, T. (1982b), 'Police and Private Security: Their Roles in Crime Prevention', *Police Review,* January, 15th., pp. 64-66, 92.

Slater, T. (1982c), 'Regulation, Standards and Goals for the Private Security Industry', *Police Review,* 26th. February, pp. 378-381.

Slynn, T. (1983), 'Blame the Police not the Crime Preventers', *Police,* September, pp. 20-22.

Smart, B. (1983), 'On Discipline and Social Regulation: A Review of Foucault's Genealogical Analysis', in Garland, D, and Young, P. (eds.), *The Power To Punish. Contemporary Penality and Social Analysis*, pp. 62-83. Heinemann, London.

Smith, D.J. (1983), *The Police and People in London*, Vol. 3, A Survey of Police Officers, Policy Studies Institute, London.

Smith, S.J. (1986), *Crime, Space and Society*, Cambridge University Press, London.

South, N. (1985), *Private Security And Social Control: The Private Security Sector In The United Kingdom, Its Commercial Functions And Public Accountability*, Ph.D. Thesis, Middlesex Polytechnic, Enfield.

South, N. (1987a), 'Law, Profit and Private Persons: Private and Public Policing in English History, in Shearing, C.D. and Stenning, P.C., (eds.), *Private Policing*, pp. 72-109, Sage, London.

South, N. (1987b), 'The Security and Surveillance of the Environment', in Lowman, J., Menzies, R. and Palys, T., *Transcarceration: Essays in the Sociology of Social Control*, pp. 139-152, Gower, Aldershot.

South, N. (1988), *Policing For Profit: The Private Security Sector*, Sage, London.

Sparks, R.F., Glenn, H. and Dodd, D.J. (1977), *Surveying Victims*, Wiley, New York.

Spitzer, S. (1981), 'The Political Economy of Policing', in Greenburg, D.F. (ed.) *Police and Capitalism*, Mayfield, London.

Spitzer, S. (1983), 'The Rationalization of Crime Control in Capitalist Society', in Cohen, S. and Scull, A.T. (eds.), *Political Control and the State: Historical and Comparative Essays*, pp. 312-333, Robertson, Oxford.

Spitzer, S. (1987), 'Security and Control in Capitalist Societies: The Fetishism of Security and the Secret Thereof' in Lowman, J., Menzies, R.J. and Palys, T.S., (eds.), *Transcarceration: Essays in the Sociology of Social Control*, pp. 43-58.

Spitzer, S. and Scull, A.T. (1977a), 'Social Control in Historical Perspective: From Private to Public Responses to Crime', in Greenberg, D.F.(ed.), *Corrections and Punishment*, pp. 265-286, Sage, Beverley Hills.

Spitzer, S. and Scull, A.T. (1977b), 'Privatisation and Capitalist Development: The Case of the Private Police', *Social Problems*, Vol. 25, No.1, pp. 18-29.

Stake, R.E. (1981), 'Case Study Methodology: An Epistemological Advocacy', in Welsh, W.W. (ed.) *Case Study Methodology in Educational Evaluation*, proceedings of the 1981 Minnesota Evaluation Conference, Minnesota Research and Evaluation Centre, Minneapolis.

Stewart, J.K. (1985), 'Public Safety and Private Police', *Public Administration Review*, No. 45, pp. 758-765.

Stuart, P.C. (1970), 'Are the Police Helped? Security Groups Gain Support but Controversy Still Smoulders', *The Christian Science Monitor*, January, 16th.

Sullivan, H.S. (1953), *Conceptions of Modern Psychiatry*, Norton, New York.

Suttles, G.D. (1972), *The Social Construction of Communities*, University of Chicago Press, Chicago.

Tanner, R.E.S. (1970), *Three Studies in East African Criminology*, Uppsala Scandinavian Institute of African Studies.

Tarling, R. and Burrows, J. (1983), 'The Work of Detectives', *Policing*, 1, pp. 57-62.

Taub, R.P. Taylor, D.G. and Dunham, J.D. (1982), *Safe and Secure Neighbourhoods: Territoriality, Solidarity, and the Reduction of Crime*, Final Report, National Institute of Justice, National Opinion Research Centre.

Taylor, I. (1979), *Justice Expenditure and Fiscal Crisis: A Working Paper*, Justice Statistics Division, Toronto.

Taylor, R.B., Gottfredson, S. and Brower, S. (1981), *Informal Control In The Urban Residential Environment*, Final Report of the National Institute for Justice, John Hopkins University Baltimore.

Thatcher, M. (1977), *Let Our Children Grow Tall*, Centre for Policy Studies, London.

Thatcher, M. (1989), A Letter To Gosforth Crime Prevention Panel Quoted in the Newcastle Evening Chronicle, 14.7.89.

The Guardian, (1989), *Private Bobbies Public Beats*, March, 8th.

Thompson, E.P. (1975), *Whigs and Hunters*, Allen Lane, London.

Tomasic, R. and Feeley, R.M. (eds.) (1982), *Neighbourhood Justice: Assessment Of An Emergency Idea*, Longman, New York.

Trevelyan, G.M. (1942), *English Social History. A Survey of Six Centuries - Chaucer to Queen Victoria*, Longmans Green and Company, London.

Trojanowicz, R.C. (1986), 'Evaluating a Neighbourhood Foot Patrol Program: The Flint, Michigan Project', in Rosenbaum, D. (ed.), *Community Crime Prevention: Does it Work?*, pp. 157-178, Sage, Beverly Hills.

Turk, A.T. (1987), 'Popular Justice and the Politics of Informalism', in Shearing, C.D. and Stenning, P.C. (eds.), *Private Policing*, pp. 131-146. Sage, London.

Tushnet, P. (1978), 'Marxist Analysis of American Law', *Marxist Perspectives*, Vol. 1, pp. 96-117.

Unger, R.M. (1976), *Law in Modern Society*, MacMillan, New York.

US Department Of Justice, (1980), *Citizen Crime Prevention Tactics: A Literature Review and Selected Bibliography*, National Institute of Justice, Washington DC.

US Private Security Advisory Council (1977), *Law Enforcement and Private Security: Areas Of Conflict Resolution*, Hallcrest Press, Virginia.

Walker, W. E., Chaiken, J.M., Jiga, A.P. and Polin, S.S. (1980), *The Impact of Proposition 13 on Local Criminal Justice Agencies: Emerging Patterns*, A Rand Note, prepared for The National Institute of Justice, U.S. Department of Justice.

Wandersman, A., Jakubs, J.F. and Giamartino, G.D. (1981), 'Participation in Block Organizations', *Journal of Community Action*, Vol. 1, pp. 40-47.

Warren, D.I. (1969), 'Neighbourhood Structure and Riot Behaviour in Detroit', *Social Problems*, Vol. 16, pp. 464-484.

Warren, D.I. (1977), 'The Functional Diversity of Urban Neighbourhoods', *Urban Affairs Quarterly*, Vol. 13, pp. 151-180.

Warren, D.I. (1978), 'Explorations in Neighbourhood Differentiation', *Sociological Quarterly*, Vol. 19, pp. 310-331.

Weatheritt, M. (1986), *Innovations in Policing*, Croom Helm, London.

Weddell, K. (1986), 'Privatizing Social Services in the U.S.A.', *Social Policy and Administration*, Vol. 20, No. 1, pp. 14-27.

Weiss, R.P. (1987), 'The Community and Prevention', in Johnson, E.H. (ed.), *Handbook on Crime and Delinquency Prevention*, pp. 113-136, Greenwood Press, New York.

West, D.J. and Farrington, D.P. (1973), *Who Becomes Delinquent?*, Heinemann, London.

Whitaker, C.J. (1986), *Crime Prevention Measures*, Bureau of Justice Statistics Special Report, US Department of Justice, Washington, DC.

White, W.T., Regan, K.J. and Wholey, J.S. (1975), *Police Burglary Prevention Programs*, US Government Printing Office, Washington DC.

Wildeman, J. (1988), *When the State Falls: A Critical Assessment of Contract Policing*, Paper Presented to the Society of Criminology, Chicago.

Williams, G. (1979), *Textbook of Criminal Law*, Sweet and Maxwell, London.

Williams, R. (1976), *Keywords*, Fontana/Croom Helm, Glasgow.

Willmott, P. (1987), *Policing and the Community*, PSI Discussion Paper No. 16, Policy Studies Institute, London.

Wilson, J.Q. and Kelling, G.L. (1982), 'Broken Windows', *The Atlantic Monthly*, March, pp. 29-38.

Wilson, J.Q. (1983), *Crime and Public Policy*, ICS Press, California.

Worsley, J. (1983), *Police,* August.

Wright, E. (1981), 'Two-Tier Policing - Can it Work? The Liverpool City Security Force', *International Security Review, October,* pp. 106-110.

Yin, R.K. (1977), *Citizen Patrol Projects,* National Evaluation Program, Summary Report, National Institute of Law Enforcement and Criminal Justice, Washington.

Yin, R.K. (1986), 'Community Crime Prevention: A Synthesis of Eleven Evaluations', in Rosenbaum, D.P., (ed.), *Community Crime Prevention: Does it Work?,* Sage, Beverly Hills.

Young, J. (1981), 'Thinking Seriously About Crime: Some Methods of Criminology', in Fitzgerald, M., McLennan, G. and Pawson, J., (eds.), *Crime and Society. Readings in History and Theory,* pp. 248-309, Routledge and Kegan Paul, London.

Young, J. (1986), 'The Failure of Criminology: The Need For A Radical Realism', in Matthews, R. and Young, J,. (Eds.), *Confronting Crime,* pp. 4-30, Sage, London.

Zimring, F.E. and Hawkins, G.J. (1973), *Deterrence: The Legal Threat in Crime Control,* University of Chicago Press, Chicago.

Index

Abel, R.L. 27
absence
  and aspects of society 40
  and bad neighbours 77, 78
  and negative factors 25
  of authority 94
  of communal spirit 76
  of legitimacy 94
  of perspective 98
  of police 57, 72, 85
active
  individualism 38-39
Adam Smith Institute 2, 32, 34
Adelman, C. 17
agency
  and structure 74, 12, 7, 132
Aitkin, M. 51
Albanese, J.S. 9, 24, 31, 71, 118
Alderson, J. 7, 108, 129, 130, 134
Aldrick, H. 51
allaying fear 25, 46, 94
  by patrol 46-47
Allen, H.E. 55
Allatt, P. 18, 28, 46, 55, 57, 65
alliance
  and regulation 134-135
Althusser, R.L. 109

Anderton, J. 108
anti collectivist 12
Arrow, K.J. 55
Ascher, K. 19, 31, 61, 64, 65
assets
  protection of 46
assurance
  and protection 97-109
Audit Commission 65, 127
authority
  absence of 94

bad neighbours
  absence of 77, 78
  economics of 77, 78
Bahan, C. 85
Bailey, S. 60
Baker, F. 51
Baker, M.H. 86
Balkin, S. 86
Barr, R. 38
Baumer, T.L. 46, 86
Bayley, D.H. 5, 8, 32
Becker, H.S. 17, 22, 124
Becker, T.M. 17, 22, 124
Becton Council 19, 65, 66, 67, 68,
  69, 70-74, 92-96, 102, 115-119

belief system 46
Belson, W.A. 28
Bennett, T.H. 27, 57, 129
Bensman, J. 124
Benson, J.K. 51
Berger, P.L. 7, 37, 73, 82, 89, 98, 118, 123, 127
Berger, B 7, 37, 73, 82, 89, 98, 118, 123
Berman, M. 121
Bittner, E. 43, 73, 98
Black, D.J. 28, 73
blurring
of policing boundaries 8, 41, 50
Boggs, S. 39, 62, 77
Boostrom, R.L. 52, 81, 106
Bottomley, K. 28, 73, 108, 129
Bottoms, A.E. 8, 122
boundary
blurring 8, 49, 50, 59
of policing 13, 18, 39, 49, 50, 108, 109
spanning 18, 108
Brady, J.P. 14
Brewer, J. 5
British Crime Survey 71
Brower, S. 39, 77
Brown, D. 97
Brown, J. 86
Buchanan, J.M. 33, 54
Burgess, E.W. 40
Burrows, J. 96, 97, 108
buying
solutions 44

Cain, M. 73
Cannell, C.F. 24
carelessness
supervision of 99, 100
Carlen, P. 35
Center, L.J. 29

Chaiken, J. 2, 8, 26, 51, 73, 108
Chaiken, M. 2, 26, 51, 73
choice
concept of 1-10, 16-19, 31-32, 117, 127
embarrassment of 127
from fate to 127
structuring 57
Clarke, R.V.G. 11, 12, 18, 27, 28, 53, 55, 56, 57, 116
class
and community 14
Clemente, F. 45
client
surveillance 98-101
Cohen, P. 9
Cohen, S. 8, 12, 13, 31, 33, 37, 39, 41, 42, 44, 47, 49, 50, 51, 52, 82, 89, 98, 109, 120, 121, 125
Coleman, C. 28, 73, 108, 129
collectivism 39, 63, 120
inactive 39, 120
Cook, K. 51
cooperation
and confrontation 50, 95, 96, 103, 108
and role conflict 52
and threat to status 106-110
concept of 46-49
frequency of 46-49, 123
of public and private police 109, 132, 135
inter-agency 52, 108, 123, 135
laissez-faire approach to 131
quality of 108, 129
Comrie, M.D. 30, 97
Conklin, J.E. 29, 80, 89
commentators
and displacement of crime 56
anti-collectivists 12
critical 35, 37, 42

on police ineffectiveness 24
revisionist 13
community
and respectable fears 80
and class consciousness 14
and the enabling state 12, 13
and the pervasive state 13, 121
and zones of neglect 42
as an ideal 38
boundaries 13
characteristics of 75-77
concept of 39-40, 63
crime rates 27-28
crime control 10, 25
crime prevention 11-13, 26, 33,
38-40, 45, 51, 53
definition of 73-75
exclusive 120
fragmentation 78-80
penetration of 8, 50
polarization 80-82
policing 32, 62, 98, 108, 119
spirit 39
surveillance of 34
symbolic 75-78
contamination
of research 27-28
Cordner, G.W. 86
Cornish, D.B. 18, 27, 28, 53, 55,
56, 57, 116
crime
as a social problem 9, 10, 14, 27,
32-33, 38, 52-55, 125-128
control and inequity 8, 53-55, 75
displacement of 7, 18-19, 28,
54-55
fear of 16, 25-27, 45-47, 82-102,
121
pattern analysis 18-19, 27-28,
110-118
recording of 28-29

statistics 28
Critchley, T. 7
Cumming, E. 30, 32, 51
Cumming, I. 30, 32
Currie, E. 80, 86
Couzens, M. 29

Dance, O.R. 130
Dean, J.P. 23, 24, 68, 69
decline
of neighbourhoods 45
Delbecq, A. 52, 108, 109, 123
demand
for order 71
Denzin, N. 10
De Sousa Santos, B. 14
Dodd, D.J. 28, 29
Donovan, E.J. 5, 25, 56, 83, 84, 97,
121
Donzelot, J. 8, 41, 133
Dunham, J.D. 39, 62, 77
Dunleavy, P. 11, 12, 33, 34, 35, 55,
56
Durkheim, E. 82

East Sussex Police 2
economic
determinism 42
freedom 53
order 34
theory of politics 34
vacuum 35-38
Edell, L. 30, 32
Edelman, M. 22
Elliott, N. 34
enabling
state 12-13
environmental design 48
Epstien, C. 32
equal provision
promoted 130

equality
  and individual freedom 8, 14
  formal 54, 127
  in policing provision 6, 9
  limitations of 132
  of justice 12, 35
  substantive 54, 127
Erikson, K. 120
ethnic minorities
  and fear of crime 18
Evan, W. M. 50
Ewan, E. 44
Ewan, S. 44
exit
  and consumer control 34, 62

Farnell, M. 3, 18, 44, 73, 98, 100,
  127
fear
  allaying of 25, 46, 97
  and community involvement 40
  and community polarization 40
  and ethnic minorities 18
  and personal victimization 66
  and property loss 81
  and psychological function 45,
  93-94
  as motivator for private patrol 66
  definition of 45-46
  of freedom 41
  perpetuation of 87-89
Feeley, R.M. 27
Fielding, N.G. 5
Foucault, M. 4, 11, 13, 49, 52, 71,
  122, 126, 128, 132, 133
Fowler, F.J. 24, 46
Fox, R.W. 45,
freedom
  of choice 47, 58, 72, 118, 126,
  127
Fromm, E. 41

frequency
  of cooperation 46-49, 123
Friedman, M. 35, 65
function of patrol
  as a key concept 43-48
  assets protection 46
  loss reduction 44
  of police 3, 33
  prevention and assurance 97-109
  sinister 89

Gabor, T. 56
Galbraith, A.J.K. 35
Gallati, R. 4
Gallup 72
Gamble, A. 53
Garland, D. 13, 20
Garofalo, J. 46, 83, 86, 88, 89, 121
George, V. 12, 35
Giamartino, G.D 39, 76
Giddens, A. 14, 20, 73, 74, 79, 82,
  89, 98, 118, 123, 132, 133, 134
Gilbert, B. 12
Gilbert, N. 12
Giller, H. 77
Gladstone, F.J. 55
Glenn, H 28, 29
Glennerster, H. 12
Goetz, J.P. 17, 18
Gottfredson, S. 39, 77
Greenberg, S.W. 39, 62, 76, 77, 89,
  121
Greenwood, P.W. 108, 129
Greer, S. 40
Guba, E.G. 18
Guest, D. 12
Gusfield, J.R. 41

Hackler, J.C. 39, 77
Hage, J. 51
Hall, S. 4, 11, 51, 80

Hamilton, P. 9
Hawkins, G.J. 53
Hayek, F.A. 11, 53, 54
Heal, K. 11
Henderson, J.H. 2, 3, 5, 12, 51, 52,
   81, 106
Herz, E.J. 27, 31, 61, 62
Hilliard, B. 119
Hirsch, F. 78
Hirschman, A.O. 2, 36, 62
Ho, K.Y. 39, 77
Holloway, J. 35
Home Office 3, 5, 30, 32, 33, 34,
   42, 43, 44, 46, 51, 58, 61, 97,
   108, 117, 119, 122, 123, 125,
   127, 129, 130, 135
Hope, T. 11, 40, 47, 61, 75, 76, 92
Hough, M. 45, 71, 72, 75
Houlden, P. 86
Hunter, A.. 39, 62, 64, 76
Huxley, A. 35
Hylton, L. 52

Ignatieff, M. 35, 37, 42, 53, 78, 118
Iles, S. 87
individualism
   and community spirit 120
   active 38, 39
inequality
   and innovation 52
   and oppression 126
   as a core value 12, 54
   of provision 6-7, 18
invasion
   of privacy 101-102
Jacobs, J. 11, 33, 48
Jakubs, J.F. 39, 76
Janowitz, M. 39, 62, 64, 76
Jayewardene, C.H.S. 128
Jefferson, T. 37
Jeffery, C.R. 48

Jenkins, D. 17
Jiga, A.P. 8
Johnson, T.J. 51, 109, 119
Jupp, V. 10
justice
   and equality 12, 35
   system of 58, 127

Kafka, F. 35, 69
Kakalik, J.S. 4
Kamenka, E. 122, 126, 128
Kasarda, J.D. 39, 62, 64, 76
Katzman, M.T. 45
Keeton, G. 123
Keller, S.I. 78, 109
Kellner, H. 7, 37, 73, 82, 89, 98,
   118, 123
Kemis, S. 17
Kirchner, R.E. 28
Kerner, H.J. 46
King, M. 11
Kings, E.J. 30, 97
Kinsey, R. 26, 38, 49, 51, 102
Klein, L. 11, 26
Kleinman, M.B. 45
Kochan, T. 51, 52, 123
knowledge 1-5, 17, 22, 40, 46, 89,
   91, 98, 120, 126
Kohfeld, C.W. 57

laissez-faire approach
   by Home Office 131-132
Lambert, J.R. 29
Latessa, E.J. 57
Lavrakas, P.J. 27, 39, 61, 62, 76
Lawler, J.M. 28
Laycock, G. 11
Lea, J. 26, 38, 49, 51, 102
Lears, T.J.J. 45
Lee, D. 36
Leifer, R. 52, 108, 109, 123

Leggett, J.C. 23
Liege, M.P. 45
Likert, R. 94
limitations
  of equality 132
Litwak, E. 52
Lenski, G.E. 23
Levine, S. 51
Lewis, H. 86
life politics
  notion of 133
  reflexive form of 134
Lilienfeld, R. 126
Lincoln, Y.S. 18
lower-class
  neighbourhoods 39, 77
Lowman, J. 13
Luckman, T. 82
Lustgarten, L. 96
Luxenburg, J. 11, 26
Lynn, G. 60

MacBarnet, D.J. 35
MacCoby, E. 24
Maguire, M. 57
Maitland, F. 124
Mangione, T.W. 46
Manning, P.K. 124
market
  solutions 74
Marplan 72
Marx, G.T. 24, 26, 48, 52, 102, 119
Mathiesen, T. 8, 13, 44, 47, 49, 52,
  120, 126, 128
Mawby, R.I. 28, 73
Maxfield, M. 27, 39, 45, 64, 76, 86,
  89, 121
Mayhew, W.P. 11, 45, 55, 71, 72,
  75
McCalla, M.E. 46
McNees, M.P. 28

Meadows, R. 134
Melossi, D. 13, 120, 128
Menchik, M.D. 8
Menzies, R.J. 13
Merry, S.E. 78, 80
Metropolitan Police 1
middle-class
  neighbourhoods 39, 77
Minar, W. 40
Minford, P. 31, 65
minimal
  policing 38
  state 13
Misner, G. 32
model
  of the public 50
Moore, C. 86
Mosca, G. 82
motivation
  and partnership 117
  and politics 121
  agent and structure 117
  as a dual process 72
market
  the 2, 6, 7, 26, 35, 58, 80, 111,
  118, 121, 127, 131, 133, 135,
motivation
  and partnership 117
  and politics 121
  as a dual process 72

Naylor, T. 30
neighbourhoods
  crime prevention in 76
  decline of 45
  less well-off 6-8
  lower-class 39, 77
  middle-class 39, 77
  research in 5
Neighbourhood Watch Scheme 61,
  62, 76

Newby, H. 38
Newcastle Journal 110
Newman, K. 108
Newman, O. 48, 81
new professionals 47
Newton, A. 46
non-situationalists 14
Normandeau, A. 57
notion
    of life-politics 133
Nowell-Smith, G. 125

O'Brien, G. 51
O'Connor, J. 9, 31, 37, 52, 62, 123
O'Higgins, M. 12
O' Leary, B. 11, 12, 33, 34, 35, 55
O'Malley, P. 52
Olson, M. 63, 64
occupational culture 2
Operational Policing Review 5, 41,
    60, 119
Oppenheim, A.N. 22, 93
order
    demand for 71
    economic 34
    public 42, 60, 72, 123
orthodox alliance 51

Packard, N. 44
Palys, T.S. 13
Pancake, D. 51
panoptical
    surveillance 46-47
Parks, E. 123
participant observation
    of patrol 26-27
Pascal, A.H. 8
Pasquino, P. 8, 133
Pate, T. 86
patrol
    allaying fear by 46-47

and exclusionary control 42
and private security 6, 25, 77
antecedents of private 59-60
in neighbourhoods 5, 6, 9
participant observation of 26-27
provision of 1
psychological effects of 83-84
public police and 5
rationale for 24-25
specific functions of 89-97
Pearson, G. 80
Pease, K. 38
penetration
    of society 46-51
Perkin, H. 79
pervasive
    state 13, 121
Petersilia, J. 108, 129
Picciotto, S. 36
Pitkin, H. 24, 120
Plant, R. 40
Platt, T. 78
police
    concept of 8
    impotency 24
    invisibility 85-86
    statistics 27-29
Police Review 5, 60
policing
    blurring of boundaries 8, 41, 50
    ineffectiveness of 6, 9, 24
    minimal 38
    overbearing system of 8, 127
    private 3, 8, 13, 30, 36, 125, 128
    provision 1, 2, 6, 15, 32, 118,
    121, 129-132
    public 3, 31, 32, 36, 50, 59, 62,
    84, 97, 118, 121
    structures 3
    territorial limits 4

policy
implications for 14, 125,
128-136
political order 34
Poulantzas, N. 35
Power, A. 12
prevention
through residential design 81
private
choice 33
private security patrol
as protection entrepreneurs 87-89
influence on public order 86-90,
93-97
in neighbourhoods 15
invasion of privacy by 101-102
non-specialized character of 100
rationale for 9, 72, 107
specific functions of 30, 43,
85-86
public
models 50
order 42, 60, 72, 123
protection 2
public choice
concept of 33-35, 54-55, 74, 82
Punch, M. 30

quality
of cooperation 108, 129

R. v Howell 95
R. v Podger 95
Radzinowicz, L. 12, 43
Randall, W. 9
rational choice 53, 56, 116
Reflexive
form of life politics 134
Regan, K.J. 54
regulation
through alliance 134-135

Reichman, N. 52
Reid, W. 51
relationships
public 4-5, 108
private 4-5, 108-109
Reppetto, T.A. 38, 56, 116
research
and case study 16-17
and ideal types 11, 14
comparative analysis 27-29
contamination 27-28
empirical 5
multi-method approach to 22
sample 21-22
triangulation 10
residential design
and prevention 81
revisionist
commentators 13
Ridley, N. 12
Rowe, C. 119
Rohe, W.M. 39, 62, 76, 77, 89, 121
role conflict
and cooperation 52-53
Rosenbaum, D.P. 78, 89, 121
Roshier, R. 11, 33, 79
Rusche, G. 13
Rutter, M. 77

Saks, M. 122
Savas, E.S. 12, 51, 61
scanning
for power 52
Schmidt, S.M. 51, 52, 123
Schnelle, J.F.K. 28
Schutz, A. 69
Scraton, P. 4, 11
Scull, A. 13, 31, 36, 52, 119
security
as intangible 121
as public corporation 132-135

as symbolic 121
emotional 44-45
inherent need for 9, 120, 129
ontological 120-122, 129, 136
Seidman, D. 29
self-help
and inter-agency cooperation 33
and neo-classicism 31-32
Seligman, B.B. 64
Sellin, T. 28
selling
solutions 44
Shapland, J. 84, 85
Shearing, C.D. 3, 4, 5, 9, 11, 13, 26,
44, 52, 73, 82, 98, 99, 100, 108,
123, 126
Sherman, L.W. 3, 11, 24, 26, 48, 51
Siatt, W. 5
situationalists
and ideology 14
sinister
state 89
Skogan, J. 27, 39, 73, 76, 79, 84,
88, 89, 128
Skolnick, J.H. 29, 108
Slater, T. 101, 109, 119, 134
Slynn, T. 9, 31, 71, 119
Smart, B. 126, 132
Smith, D.J. 97
Smith, T.G. 29
Smith, S.J. 45
social control
and policing
and the state 44-47, 52
disciplinary form of 8, 122
informal 11, 33
sinister forms of 50
theory of
social institutions
and the state 8, 30

society
and equality 6
and policing structures 3, 37
insurance for 132-133
modern 20-21, 127
of strangers 79
penetration of 46-51
security for 132-133
solutions
buying 44
selling 44
market 74
South, N. 4, 5, 7, 8, 9, 13, 20, 25,
30, 43, 82
Sparks, R.F. 28, 29
Sprague, J. 57
Spitzer, S. 7, 13, 31, 34, 36, 44, 45,
52, 62, 80, 119, 121
Stake, R.E. 17
status
threat to 106-110
Stewart, J.K. 24
structure
and agency 74, 137, 132
Stuart, P.C. 81
substantive
equality 54, 127
Sullivan, H.S. 120
surveillance
and control 122-123
client 98-101
extrusion 48-50
failure of 54
innocuous 102-103
intrusion 48-50
offender 98-99
panoptical 46-47
Suttles, G.D. 24, 41, 42, 63, 80, 81,
120

Tanner, R.E.S. 28

Takagi, P. 78
Tarling, R. 97, 108
Taub, R.P. 39, 62, 77
Tay, A.E. 122, 126, 128
Taylor, D.G. 39, 62, 77
Taylor, I. 35
Taylor, R.B. 39, 77
territorial attitude
   and community 40
the market
   and freedom 35
   and policing 2, 6
Thatcher, M. 31, 32, 54
The Guardian 60
the state
   enabling 11-13
   minimal 13
theory
   capitalist logic 10, 35
   classicism 12, 56, 127
   conservatism 12, 54
   defensible space 58
   left-functionalism 118
   neo-classicism 10-12
   public choice 32-35, 54-56, 74
   rational choice 18-19, 53, 56-57,
   116
Thompson, E.P. 70
threat
   to status 106-110
Tomasic, R. 27
Travers, T. 12
Travis, L.F. 55
Trevelyan, G.M. 2
triangulation
   as research method 10
Trojanowicz, R.C. 86
Turk, A.T. 38, 39, 76
Tushnet, P. 35
Tullock, G. 33

Unger, R.M. 109, 124
Urquhart-Ross, C. 39, 77
US Department of Justice 46

Vagg, J. 84, 85
voice
   and consumer control 34

Walker, W. E. 8
Walsh, W.F. 5, 25, 46, 83, 84, 97,
   121
Wandersman, A. 39, 76
Warren, D.I. 24, 40, 41, 42
Weatheritt, M. 97
Weddell, K. 12
Weiss, R.P. 40, 42
West, D.J. 28, 60
White, P.E. 51, 57, 105
White, W.T. 54
Whyte, W.F. 23, 24, 68, 69
Wildhorn, S. 4
Wilding, P. 12, 35
Williams, G. 95
Williams, J.R. 39, 62, 76, 77, 89,
   121
Wilson, J.Q. 11, 12, 32, 86
Whitaker, C.J. 76
Wholey, J.S. 54, 55
Wildeman, J. 119
Willmott, P. 40
Wolfgang, M. 28
Worsley, J. 75
Wright, E. 128
Wycoff, M.A. 76

Yin, R.K. 46, 78
Young, J. 11, 12, 26, 38, 49, 51
Young, P. 13, 70

Zimring, F.E. 53
zones of neglect 42

For Product Safety Concerns and Information please contact our EU
representative GPSR@taylorandfrancis.com
Taylor & Francis Verlag GmbH, Kaufingerstraße 24, 80331 München, Germany

* 9 7 8 1 0 3 2 8 1 7 2 5 5 *